Unfathomable

The Miracles of Jesus Say

You Matter

TERRY K. LANFORD

○

Contents

Introduction

God Is Unfathomable

I find numerous aspects of our existence impossible to wrap my mind around. Even with insights and discoveries by brilliant people who've provided answers, some realities still overwhelm because of their complexity and magnitude. One example is the size of the universe.

At the Space.com website, Nola Taylor Redd tells us this:

> Like a ship in the empty ocean, astronomers on Earth can turn their telescopes to peer 13.8 billion light-years in every direction, which puts Earth inside of an *observable* sphere with a radius of 13.8 billion light-years. The word "observable" is key; the sphere limits what scientists can see but not what is there. ("How Big Is the Universe?"; *https://www.space.com/24073-how-big-is-the-universe.html*)

Let 13.8 billion light-years sink into your thoughts, then contemplate what is beyond that can't be seen. If that doesn't stretch your synapses, you might stand on a mountaintop or on a beach and contemplate the rotation of the earth on its axis, or the earth's tilt and path around the sun. Should you desire to really make your head spin, research the parameters of our planet necessary to sustain life. Maybe you have an aptitude for biology and chemistry; in that case, maybe you should study the amazing biological functions in the human body.

My point is that we live in a universe full of mystery, unexplored horizons, and mind-boggling realities far beyond our understanding. I believe this points to the intelligent design of a creator, and that creator is the God of the Bible. The Bible tells us that this God is unfathomable:

> Your knowledge is beyond my comprehension; it is so far beyond me, I am unable to fathom it. (Psalm 139:6)

> When I look at your heavens, the work of your fingers, the moon and the stars, which you have set in place, what is man that you are mindful of him, and the son of man that you care for him? Yet you have made him a little lower than the heavenly beings and crowned him with glory and honor. (Psalm 8:3-8)

> The LORD looks down from heaven; he sees all the children of man; from where he sits enthroned he looks out on all the inhabitants of the earth. (Psalm 33:13-14)

Have you not known? Have you not heard? The LORD is the everlasting God, the Creator of the ends of the earth. He does not faint or grow weary; his understanding is unsearchable. (Isaiah 40:28)

Can you find out the deep things of God? Can you find out the limit of the Almighty? It is higher than heaven—what can you do? Deeper than Sheol—what can you know? (Job 11:7-8)

I will extol you, my God and King, and bless your name forever and ever. Every day I will bless you and praise your name forever and ever. Great is the LORD, and greatly to be praised, and his greatness is unsearchable. (Psalm 145:3)

In that last line, David describes God's greatness as unsearchable. God's knowledge is so far beyond human comprehension that David says he is unable to fathom it: "Such knowledge is too wonderful for me; it is high; I cannot attain it" (Psalm 139:6).

What is true of David's inability to fathom God is true also of all finite humans. Along with David, we ask, "What is man that you are mindful of him, and the son of man that you care for him?" (Psalm 8:3-8).

Job asks, "Can you probe the limits of God?" The obvious answer is no. Who can explain the infinite God? Who can comprehend the God who is everlasting? How can anyone wrap their finite human mind around the Being who is all-knowing and omnipresent? How are we to grasp the One who said, "Let there be light"—and there was light (Genesis 1:3)? How can we comprehend the One who placed the moon and stars in the heavens?

While God is unfathomable in all His attributes, what is most unfathomable about Him is the love He displayed in and through the incarnation of His Son, Jesus. Do you know the story of His unfathomable love? "In the beginning was the Word, and the Word was with God, and the Word was God" (John 1:1). Jesus is the word. "And the Word became flesh and dwelt among us, and we have seen his glory, glory as of the only Son from the Father, full of grace and truth" (1:14). God's love moved Him to send His Son to rescue and redeem lost people. "For God so loved the world, that he gave his only Son, that whoever believes in him should not perish but have eternal life" (3:16).

Do you find it unfathomable that "God shows his love for us in that while we were still sinners, Christ died for us" (Romans 5:8)? God stands with open arms, ready to welcome anyone who will turn from sin and self and confess Jesus as Lord.

When Jesus became flesh and walked this earth, His attributes of deity were on display in His words and works. The miracles Jesus performed are unfathomable. Even more unfathomable are His mercy, compassion, and love displayed in each miracle story. Jesus always accomplishes much more than meets the eye through His signs and wonders.

With every miracle, God brings about changes in circumstances that are beyond human understanding or explanation. The physical implications or results of a miracle can be described, but the supernatural power that brought about the result cannot be explained.

Miracles are beyond explanation. If we could explain how God performed the unfathomable, these events wouldn't be miracles, and God would not be God. What we can do is seek to understand the why. When we do, we witness boundless compassion, love, and mercy. We discover Jesus accomplishing much more than signs and wonders. We also recognize that His displays of deity are meant to move us to greater faith, greater love for one another, and lives of more devoted discipleship.

The magnitude of any specific miracle of Jesus cannot be measured by a perceived degree of impossibility. No numeric value could be assigned to walking on water or calming a storm. The magnitude I hope to draw your attention to has to do with eternal consequences. I invite you to join me as we explore some of what Jesus accomplished (we could never explore it all) in the lives of those who were touched by His signs and wonders.

On the fringes of the supernatural, we find the startling, astonishing, and unfathomable. We also discover the comforting and reassuring.

This book is not for those interested in a theological treatment of the miracles of Jesus. The reader I have in mind is the single mom with three kids who's struggling to make ends meet, or the senior adult living alone and battling health problems. My prayer is that this book will provide encouragement to the couple struggling with their marriage, or to parents of rebellious children. I'm thinking also of the person whose spouse is shackled by a crippling addiction. This book is for people living ordinary lives with challenges that have caused them to pray for God's supernatural intervention.

Together, what can we learn from the miracles of Christ? Please join me as we explore His miracles and discover spiritual lessons for believers today.

I suspect that the two questions most often asked by people regarding the miracles of Jesus are something like these:

1. Does Jesus still perform miracles today?

2. How can I get Jesus to perform a miracle in my life?

I'll attempt to answer these questions, but let me state at the outset that we need to consider our motivations for asking the second question. I'll say more about those motivations in a moment.

The answer to the first question is an emphatic yes. There's a lengthy theological answer, but I'm going to offer a short foundational truth for you to consider. The author of the book of Hebrews tells us that Jesus created all things and that He is presently upholding or sustaining those things by the word of His power (Hebrews. 1:2-3). Paul said in Colossians 1:17 that Jesus is before all things, and in Him all things are held together. Now that's a miracle. So yes, Jesus is still performing miracles today. He's not only holding the world together so we have a planet to live on, He's also doing infinitely more. Jesus has the power to perform supernatural things in our lives.

This leads to the second question, which is much more personal. You may be in the midst of overwhelming challenges right now, and in your desperation you see a miracle as your only way out. I understand those feelings. On the other hand, you may be asking for a miracle because, based on the evidence you see, you don't believe in the miracles of God that already exist.

We must be careful here to remember a warning from Jesus: "Unless you see signs and wonders you will not believe" (John 4:48).The Greek word for "you" in this verse is plural. He's talking to everyone standing there. We'll dig into this a little deeper when we look at how Jesus miraculously healed an official's son, but Jesus is addressing those who keep demanding miracles and still won't believe.

In the miracle stories, faith in Christ comes before the miracle. Faith is trust that flows from a relationship. Asking for a miracle without first having the relationship is like saying, "I want the miracle, but that's all I want of you." Approaching Jesus from such a selfish perspective will never bring about His supernatural intervention in your circumstances.

Some words from the apostle James about our motives in asking for things in prayer must also be remembered:

"You ask and do not receive, because you ask wrongly, to spend it on your passions" (James 4:3). Our approach to the miracles of Christ must first and foremost be motivated by a desire to learn more about Christ, to grow in our faith, and to become more like Him.

Every miracle Jesus performed points to His deity. Whether He spoke to the wind, rebuked demons, walked on water, turned water to wine, or raised the dead, His attributes of deity were on display. I hope you'll keep this in mind with each miracle we survey. The evidence of His deity is just one reason the Holy Spirit has provided the eyewitness accounts of these marvelous events. As we study individual miracles, I ask you to consider what Jesus did beyond the demonstration of His supernatural power. Jesus accomplished so much more than the obvious supernatural event. He was and is the ultimate multitasker.

Keep in mind that Jesus was training disciples. He was not only teaching those who were physically present with Him, but also those who would come after. He was teaching them about sincere faith. He was demonstrating His immense love and compassion which believers are to emulate. Jesus was building disciples who would soon turn the world upside down and become the church.

Before we begin with the miracles, I want to explain a concept I call compassionate disciple-making.

Showing compassion makes me feel vulnerable. I'm embarrassed to admit that although I'm passionate about teaching God's Word, I haven't always blended my passion with great compassion for people. I've operated under the premise that the best thing I can do for people is pray for them and teach them from the Word. I've sought to channel my compassion through giving to a worthy cause, going on mission trips to share the gospel, or sending an encouraging card. Frankly, I've been afraid of caring too much, because the problems of others are messy and time-consuming. I have my own problems to address. I've even fought the urge to care, saying to myself, "Don't get involved."

My rationalization has been that the best use of my time and gifts is to teach. I've sought to teach others the Bible, theology, doctrine, spiritual disciplines, study methods, lesson preparation, models of discipleship—the list goes on. The Scriptures confirm that knowledge of God and God's Word is essential to living the Christian life. Yet recently I've been confronted with the hypocrisy of my thinking, actions, and excuses. Jesus not only taught the disciples with words for three years, but also cared for people along the way. Allowing His followers to see His compassion translated into action was as much a part of His teaching as the words He used.

Jesus commanded that we go and make disciples (Matthew 28:18-20), but He also commanded that we love one another (John 13:34-35). He washed the feet of His disciples to demonstrate how they were to serve each other (John 13:1-17). His entire life was about sacrifice for those He loved. This verse bears repeating: "God shows His love for us in that while we were sinners, Christ died for us" (Romans 5:8).

During a conversation with a friend about Bible teachers incorporating certain aspects of disciple-making into their Bible study lessons, my friend reminded me of an important truth: "What do people remember from a lesson after a few days?" Then he pointed out that people never forget when you were there for them in a difficult time, or even in small ways when you showed interest in their lives.

This brought to my mind the old adage, "They don't care how much you know until they know how much you care." I began to remember tough situations in ministry where I prayed with people during times of crisis. I thought of times when I was present for important events in life such as weddings, births, or surgeries. Occasionally I'll bump into people who'll thank me for when I was "there" for them. I've learned that those moments of living out concern and genuine compassion create greater openness and trust.

For three years, the disciples heard Jesus teach many times. They heard His Sermon on the Mount, His discourse on the bread of life, His parables, His conversations with individuals, and His confrontations with religious leaders. They witnessed others respond in amazement to what Jesus said and the authority with which He said it. Jesus was making His disciples into "fishers of men" (Matthew 4:9)—and a central component of that process was learning Christlike compassion. His compassion was on visual display for the woman who poured expensive perfume on His feet. His compassion is the reason He didn't condemn the woman caught in adultery. His compassion was why He conversed with the woman at the well. Seeing Jesus display compassion was central to His men becoming disciples.

No matter what model of discipleship you prefer, and there are many, we must acknowledge that each model is incomplete without compassion. Loving God and being imitators of Christ will mean that we must reflect His compassionate character.

The lessons for followers of Christ regarding the essentials of compassion are possibly most evident in the miracles of Jesus. The circumstances surrounding His signs and wonders also serve as lessons in compassionate disciple-making.

Join me as we walk through the miracles of Christ and seek to learn what His Spirit will reveal about growing in Christlikeness. Let's witness together His love and compassion—and adopt His model of building compassionate disciples.

1

Miracle: Jesus Turns Water into Wine

Read John 2:1–11

Not long ago, my daughter's wedding taught my wallet a painful lesson. Weddings can be elaborate and expensive affairs. People in the US spend thousands of dollars to create the perfect storybook setting for that special moment. The venue must be picturesque. The dresses and flower arrangements must be spectacular. The caterer strives to provide the most delicious meal for the reception. The kind of simple serving of nuts, punch, and cake that was served at my wedding is considered an embarrassment today.

The setting for Jesus's first miracle was a Jewish wedding in Cana of Galilee. The names of the bride and bridegroom aren't given, but whoever they were, they had an embarrassing problem on one of the most special days of their young lives.

Mary, the mother of Jesus, approached Him and said, "They have no wine" (John 2:3). Her statement, while not an outright request, certainly implied that Jesus could do something to help. Jesus understood what His mother was asking, and He asked, "Woman, what does this have to do with me? My hour has not yet come" (2:4).

Mary didn't plead with Jesus to reconsider, nor did she attempt to explain the seriousness of the problem. She simply instructed the servants to do whatever Jesus said. Her response reveals her absolute confidence in whatever Jesus decided to do.

Do *you* have absolute confidence in the plans Jesus has for you?

Notice what happened next.

> Now there were six stone water jars there for the Jewish rites of purification, each holding twenty or thirty gallons. Jesus said to the servants, "Fill the jars with water." And they filled them up to the brim. And he said to them, "Now draw some out and take it to the master of the feast." So they took it. When the master of the feast tasted the water now become wine, and did not know where it came from (though the servants who had drawn the water knew), the master of the feast called the bridegroom and said to him, "Everyone serves the good wine first, and when people have drunk freely, then the poor wine. But you have kept the good wine until now." (John 2:6-10)

Because of the strong cultural expectations of that day, running out of wine at a wedding was hugely embarrassing and could have led to the taking back of wedding gifts. This was not the way a couple wanted to start a marriage.

Sitting close by were six stone water jars. Each held twenty to thirty gallons of water to be used in ceremonial washing. Servants poured water from these jars into a basin so guests could wash their hands and arms before eating. While the washing may have been good hygiene, the Jews placed great significance on this religious ritual as a way to purify oneself before God. Anyone using these jars for another purpose would temporarily be defiled.

Yet Jesus transformed the water in these jars into wine.

If the guests had known the wine came from those jars, they might well have been deeply offended and refused to touch it. Jesus, however, showed more concern for this couple's wedding than for contemporary ritual.

The master of the banquet said the best wine was supposed to be served first. The wine Jesus provided was exceptional.

Jesus met a material need by providing wine, but the symbolism behind this miracle is much greater. While compassionately showing a young couple unexpected grace by meeting their need, Jesus displayed a wonderful truth. Jesus was the true master of the banquet, just as He will be one day at the marriage supper of the Lamb. With supernatural intervention, Jesus transformed those ordinary vessels into something incredibly valuable. And He desires to do the same in our lives.

This story presents a powerful allegory for Jesus's saving grace. Those attending the wedding were practicing a washing ritual that would never cleanse them internally or spiritually. The wine is a picture of the blood of Jesus that offers true soul cleansing, not just ceremonial washing. What a beautiful picture of the new covenant, which Jesus was about to initiate by going to the cross!

This event is often referred to as the first of His seven signs of deity found in the book of John. Jesus instantly converted around one hundred twenty gallons of water into wine. What does that mean to me? It means that He has the power to meet any need in my life. I'm reminded of this promise: "My God will supply every need of yours according to his riches in glory in Christ Jesus" (Philippians 4:19).

Many years ago, my wife was lead to go on a mission trip to Romania. We prayed together, and we asked God to meet our financial needs. When she originally committed to go, our finances were in decent shape. But we were then surprised with unexpected expenses, and we began to wonder how we could pay for the trip.

My wife was a nurse and worked different shifts. Very near the time we were to make the final payment, she came home from work one evening and told me her employer had discovered a shift differential that she was due going back several months. The check was in the *exact* amount of the cost of the trip. God is able!

Questions for Reflection

1. The servants cooperated with Jesus by bringing the jars and filling them with water. What was the result? What does that mean for servants of Christ today?

2. What significance might there be in Jesus using these particular jars (which were used in Jewish purification rites) as containers for the new wine He created?

3. What does this miracle mean to you?

2

Miracle: Jesus Heals an Official's Son

Read John 4:43-54

My wife and I have experienced the anguish of seeing one of our children in terrible agony. We know what it is to feel totally helpless to ease the immediate suffering of a loved one.

My daughter was two years old when a waitress spilled a freshly brewed pot of steaming hot coffee onto our little girl's lap and legs. I was in the restroom when I heard her screaming and crying. By the time I got to the table, my wife had her out of the high chair, and in moments we were racing down the road to the emergency room and praying. Thank God for the skills He has given doctors and nurses and for medication that eases pain and heals wounds. Although the healing process was difficult, our baby recovered. She was left with a few small scars.

The apostle John tells the story of a father who was desperate and panicked, consumed with fear for his son's life. The father traveled twenty miles to meet with someone he'd heard could perform miracles. This nobleman, a man of means, didn't send a servant or another member of his household to Jesus; he came in person. The nobleman would spare nothing to save the life of his son.

Can you relate? Who wouldn't seek out the best doctor or hospital to save his or her child?

Jesus told him, "Unless you see signs and wonders, you will not believe" (John 4:48). The word translated "you" here is plural; Jesus is talking to everyone present.

Crowds were following Him because they'd heard about the miracles Jesus had performed, or had seen these wonders for themselves. Some came for the show, while others came because of curiosity. Many in the crowed wanted to be near someone popular. They came to be wowed.

But not this nobleman. He came with a desperate need, as he made clear to Jesus: "Sir, come down before my child dies" (John 4:49). This father, who wasn't used to begging for anything, pleaded with Jesus to travel to his house and heal his son. He believed Jesus could do it, but not from a distance.

Knowing what He was about to do for this father, Jesus essentially asked, "Will you take Me at My word?" This was a test of faith. Would the official believe without seeing?

Jesus wants to build a belief that comes from devotion—a faith that trusts in His Word.

"Go," Jesus told the man. "Your son will live."

Then John tells us, "The man believed the word that Jesus spoke to him and went on his way" (4:50).

Before this father believed, I imagine he stood there for a few heartbeats, processing what Jesus had said to him, wondering how best to respond. Jesus hadn't said what this nobleman wanted to hear. But there was no questioning the words of Christ. Through this desperate father's complete acceptance and trust, he received the promise of Jesus:

> As he was going down, his servants met him and told him that his son was recovering. So he asked them the hour when he began to get better, and they said to him, "Yesterday at the seventh hour the fever left him." The father knew that was the hour when Jesus had said to him, "Your son will live." And he himself believed, and all his household. (John 4:51-53)

The miracle of turning water into wine had happened in an instant, which demonstrates that Jesus is Lord over time. The healing of this official's son happened in an instant also, but over a long distance. Jesus is also Lord over space.

Ultimately our faith comes down to whether we'll accept the words of Jesus as truth. Do we believe His promises, and will we act on them? The Bible is full of promises from our Lord. Will you take Him at His word?

Questions for Reflection

1. Notice how Jesus said "Go" to the official just before He said, "your son will live"? What do you think Jesus was communicating by this command?

2. Why was it important for the official to learn the exact time when his son began to get better?

3. What does this miracle reveal concerning the promises of Jesus?

3

Miracle: Jesus Drives out an Evil Spirit

Read Mark 1:21-27; Luke 4:31-36

What's the most unusual interruption you've experienced during a worship service? One Sunday morning I was enjoying praise and worship in a church which was equipped with bright lights, wonderful acoustics, and bright video screens when the electricity suddenly went off. Standing with the crowd in that dark and quiet sanctuary was eerie for a few moments. Thankfully, after a few moments the emergency lights came on, and we continued to worship.

I've also experience unfortunate interruptions in worship services because people suffered a medical crisis. And in one worship service, I saw a person stand and shout in the middle of the service.

Unexpected interruptions in worship gets everyone's attention.

Mark tells of an unusual interruption to a worship service. On this particular Sabbath, while Jesus was teaching, a man possessed by an unclean spirit cried out,

"What have you to do with us, Jesus of Nazareth? Have you come to destroy us? I know who you are—the Holy One of God." Jesus rebuked him, saying, "Be silent, and come out of him!" (Mark 1:24-25). During many of His encounters with demons, Jesus commanded them to keep silent.

Two key words in this passage are especially important for understanding the events taking place here. The first word is *astonished*. It's a word used elsewhere to describe how people in Jesus's day reacted to His teaching. We read that "the crowds were astonished" by the teaching Jesus gave in the Sermon on the Mount (Matthew 7:28).

Even though Jesus was ultimately rejected in hometown of Nazareth, when He taught in their synagogue the people "were astonished, and said, "Where did this man get this wisdom and these mighty works? Is not this the carpenter's son? Is not his mother called Mary? And are not his brothers James and Joseph and Simon and Judas?'" (Matthew 13:54-55). We also read of a time when His disciples likewise "were astonished at His words" (Mark 10:24 NKJV). Much earlier, when Jesus was a boy asking questions of the teachers in the temple in Jerusalem, we read that "all who heard Him were astonished at His understanding and answers" (Luke 2:47 NKJV).

The teaching of Jesus was astonishing because its content is profound and reveals a supernatural genius that comes only from God.

A second key word from this story of Jesus driving out an evil spirit is *authority*. The people in the synagogue were astonished at Jesus because "He taught them as one who had authority, and not as the scribes" (Mark 1:22). Jesus gave them a lesson about the extent of His authority they likely never forgot.

In other accounts in Scripture where Jesus allowed demons to speak, they asked Him what He had to do with them—in other words, why He'd come there. A second thing the demons asked was whether He had come to destroy or torment them. On one occasion they asked, "Have you come here to torment us before the time?"—and they even asked Him that day to send them into a group of pigs (Matthew 8:28-31).

Not only did demons recognize Jesus, but they also understood His authority and power over them. They referred to Him as the Son of God or the Holy One of God. As we're told in James 2:19, "You believe that there is one God. Good! Even the demons believe that—and shudder."

In the synagogue that day when Jesus drove out the evil spirit, imagine the people's expressions and thoughts when they witnessed the power of Jesus over the unseen spiritual realm:

> And they were all amazed, so that they questioned among themselves, saying, "What is this? A new teaching with authority! He commands even the unclean spirits and they obey him." (Mark 1:27)

Both His words and His works display the authority of Jesus Christ.

Jesus spoke often about the nature of His authority. Moments before He gave what we call the Great Commission, Jesus said, "All authority in heaven and on earth has been given to me" (Matthew 28:17). This is the highest, most powerful, and most perfect authority that exists.

On another occasion, Jesus said in regard to His life, "No one takes it from me, but I lay it down of my own accord. I have authority to lay it down, and I have authority to take it up again. This charge I have received from my Father" (John 10:18).

Knowing that Jesus has absolute authority should be a great comfort for us. We know He has authority over powers of darkness and evil. He has authority to fulfill every promise He has made of peace, comfort, and eternity for those who belong to Him. We can rest assured that "for those who love God, all things work together for good" (Romans 8:28).

If we want to experience a walk of faithful obedience and blessing, we must recognize and respond to the authority of Jesus.

Are you submitting your will to His perfect will?

Questions for Reflection

1. What are the implications of the demonized man's question: "What have you to do with us, Jesus of Nazareth?"

2. Why did Jesus command the demon to be silent?

3. Paul says in Ephesians 6 that every believer faces spiritual warfare. How does the power of Jesus over the unseen spirit world impact your view of spiritual warfare?

4

Miracle: Jesus Heals Peter's Mother-in-Law

Read Matthew 8:14-15; Mark 1:29-31; Luke 4:38-39

After an amazing church service in Capernaum, Simon Peter invited Jesus to his house.

Now that's a novel idea! How many times have we left Jesus at church?

Upon entering Simon's home, Jesus learned that Simon's mother-in-law had a high fever. In Luke 4:38, we read that the people near her sickbed "appealed to him on her behalf."

This story helps us understand the extreme importance of interceding in prayer on behalf of others in need. Parallel accounts of this story in Matthew 8 and Mark 1 reveal that Jesus bent over Simon's mother-in-law and took her hand. Aren't you glad our Savior is willing to bend toward us and take our hand?

Jesus then rebuked the fever. And Simon's mother-in-law immediately got up and began to serve those who were there.

The story of this woman's healing is brief. If you look for a lot of details about what happened, you'll be disappointed. This miracle is barely mentioned. After two or three verses, the Gospel writers move ahead to describe the next event. While this miracle may appear almost insignificant, we must remember it certainly wasn't insignificant to Peter's mother-in-law—nor to many others who heard what had happened and then went to find Jesus.

After sundown, when the Sabbath was over and the Jews were again allowed to carry burdens, people lined up outside Simon Peter's door. "Now when the sun was setting, all those who had any who were sick with various diseases brought them to him, and he laid hands on every one of them and healed them" (Luke 4:40). Jesus healed them all!

When Jesus is invited into our homes, He compassionately helps us with our burdens. He brings supernatural power to bless us. Having Jesus in the home brings about an overflow that will impact the surrounding community.

Through your submission to God's Spirit and His Word, you may be the instrument through which He spiritually heals your neighbors and friends.

Questions for Reflection

1. What do you think about the response of Peter's mother-in-law to her healing?

2. What does healing someone of a high fever suggest when compared to raising someone from the dead?

3. Do you use your home as a place to host others who have needs?

5

Miracle: The First Miraculous Catch of Fish

Read Luke 5:1-11

What's the greatest step of faith you've ever taken? I'm talking about a scary step into the unknown, when you thought, "If Jesus doesn't show up in this situation, I'm facing a risky and uncertain outcome."

For some people, that step was sharing a devotion with a small group for the first time. For others it was the first time they told someone about their relationship with Jesus. That step might have been a decision to go on a short-term mission trip or to leave a secular career to engage in full-time ministry.

After spending twenty years working in business and industry, I took a life-altering step of faith to pursue pastoral ministry. Years later, I experienced another life-altering step as I was reassigned to a parachurch ministry of equipping. Those steps of faith meant huge changes for my family and me. I know from experience that the call to launch out into the deep and unknown can be a frightening experience.

The miracle of the first catch of fish happened early in Jesus's ministry, as He was calling His first disciples. The miracle is unusual in that Simon wasn't looking for a miracle. Jesus interrupted Simon's intended short-term future (to go home and get some sleep) with a strange request. After teaching the people from the boat, Jesus turned to Simon and said, "Put out into the deep and let down your nets for a catch" (Luke 5:4).

Not only was the request strange, but it contradicted everything Simon's previous night's experience said was reasonable. Simon's reality was that the fish weren't there.

Do Simon's thoughts resonate with you? Simon clearly thought the effort would be a waste. I imagine he thought, "Are you serious? We've been fishing all night and haven't caught a thing. Besides, we just now cleaned our nets!" What he actually said was, "Master, we have toiled all night and took nothing! But at your word I will let down the nets" (Luke 5:5). I wonder if Simon thought, "Rather than argue with Jesus, I'll just go along to prove my point."

Simon and those with him launched out into the deep and lowered their nets. The result was an unfathomable and mind-boggling miracle—nets so full of fish that the boats began to sink.

Simon and his partners James and John were astonished by the catch. Simon fell at the feet of Jesus and said, "Depart from me, for I am a sinful man, O Lord" (5:8). Jesus invited these men to follow Him, and they left everything to do so.

In Matthew's Gospel, we find a little different wording of Jesus's invitation to follow Him. The wording gives us greater insight into the reason for this miracle. Jesus said, "Follow Me, and I will make you become fishers of men" (Matthew 4:19). Please note the manner in which these disciples would become fishers of men; the key phrase Jesus used is "I will make you…" Twelve men would follow Jesus for the next three years. They'd listen to His teaching and watch His actions, which would be the basis for their spiritual formation.

Like those disciples, we must be willing to sit at the feet of the Master so that He can make us into disciples who are fishers of men.

Jesus desires all His followers will leave behind a shallow faith that hangs near the security of the shore and to launch out into the deep water of faith—where the fishing is best. Deep faith will yield blessings so tremendous that we'll barely be able to contain them.

Do you honestly desire a spiritual yield in your life so large that you would need to beg for help in handling the overflow? If so, launch out into the deep water in your prayer life, in studying the Word, and in sharing the good news with others.

There's a stunning acceleration in spiritual rewards when we walk in deep faith and allow Jesus to show us where to fish. When we heed the words of our Lord no matter how far out they seem, the results will be unfathomable.

Questions for Reflection

1. Why did Simon agree to move his boat into the deep?

2. Why did Jesus perform this miracle?

3. This miraculous catch of fish happened at the beginning of Jesus's three years with the disciples. What's the significance of the timing of this miracle?

6

Miracle: Jesus Cleanses a Man of Leprosy

Read Matthew 8:2-4; Mark 1:40-45; Luke 5:12-16

The bestseller *Fifty Shades of Grey* is an erotic romance novel that has been made into a popular movie. The title is intriguing. I don't know what the author intended, but the title caused me to think of a steady progression into darkness or varying degrees of morality. From a purely human perspective, we might look at the various acts of evil that people do to one another and call them "shades of depravity."

Do you sometimes see news reports and wonder how people can do such horrible things? Murder. Kidnapping. Sexual assault and abuse. Gang violence. What's wrong with humanity? How can people be so cruel to each other? At the same time, we might well consider the sins present in our own lives.

The truth is that there exists in every human being the same nature that leads to terrible evils. That nature is called a sin nature, and it's highly contagious. In fact, it's passed along to every single human born into this world.

In Jesus's day, leprosy was a contagious disease with no known cure. In healing a leper, Jesus again did the unfathomable—while teaching us about His power over sin.

In Luke 5:12-16, a man with leprosy approached Jesus and said, "Lord, if you will, you can make me clean." This man recognized his need. He was aware of his condition. And although leprosy was so contagious and incurable, Jesus touched this man and said, "I will; be clean."

Jesus didn't have to touch this leper in order to heal him. Can you imagine the looks on the faces of the disciples as Jesus touched him? According to Jewish law, this made Jesus unclean. What a compassionate and profound gesture! Jesus was expressing mercy by His willingness to take on this dreadful and dangerous disease. He stepped into the messiness and brokenness of this man's life, and in doing so He demonstrated His willingness to become sin for us, that we might be healed: "God shows his love for us in that while we were still sinners, Christ died for us" (Romans 5:8).

Jesus stands ready to step into your broken and messy life. He's willing to touch you with His healing touch and to cleanse you with His redeeming blood. Unfathomable!

Our sin nature is much like leprosy. In fact, we're all spiritual lepers. Our condition prevents us from entering into the presence of God because He cannot look upon sinful man (Psalm 5:5; Habakkuk 1:13; Revelation 21:27).

There's only one cure. Like the leper in Luke 5, we must go to Jesus for cleansing. We can confidently approach Him with all our need, sin, and defilement. He will not turn us away (Hebrews 4:16; Psalm 103:12). On the contrary, He has promised believers the indwelling presence of His Holy Spirit to help us in our spiritual battle against temptation and sin (Galatians 5:16).

Questions for Reflection

1. After healing this man, why did Jesus tell him to tell no one?

2. Why did Jesus command the man to show himself to the priest and make an offering for his cleansing?

3. The law demanded that lepers keep their distance from other people. What does this man's posture before Jesus and His willingness to break the law tell you about his belief concerning Jesus?

7

Miracle: Jesus Heals a Centurion's Servant

Read Matthew 8:5-13; Luke 7:1-10

Jesus often amazed people with His words and actions, but only once does Scripture reveal that Jesus Himself was amazed by someone's faith. That someone wasn't even Jewish, but a Roman centurion who appealed to Jesus on behalf of one of his servants. He was part of the conquering and occupying force that held Israel in bondage.

As a Gentile, this man was considered unclean by the Jews, and therefore unworthy to receive blessings from Yahweh. Yet this man had earned a good reputation because he showed favor to the Jews by assisting them in building a synagogue. The centurion's assistance led the elders of the Jews to appeal to Jesus on this man's behalf.

The timing of this miracle, which occurred shortly after the famous Sermon on the Mount, is significant. Matthew 5–7 recounts this famous sermon in which Jesus addressed many topics. He said that a child of God seeks the righteousness of God and is humble. A true follower of God is repentant over sin, loves even his enemies, and is merciful. Jesus contrasted this kind of true discipleship with the Jewish religious leaders, who were self-righteous, condemning, and judgmental without mercy. They sought their own glory rather than God's. Jesus told His listeners, "Unless your righteousness exceeds that of the scribes and Pharisees, you will never enter the kingdom of heaven" (Matthew 5:20).

Against this backdrop, the Roman centurion came to Jesus and appealed on behalf of his servant— "who was sick and at the point of death" (Luke 7:2). This Roman provides a startling contrast in heart to the Jewish religious leaders. The story reveals amazing aspects of his love for others and his view of Jesus:

1. The centurion's love for his slave was amazing. Luke tells us that this servant "was highly valued by him" (7:2). The word translated "highly regarded," *entimos*, also means "precious."

2. The centurion's love for his enemies was amazing. The Jews hated the pagan Roman occupation of their precious promised land. Yet they considered this centurion to be a worthy man because he helped build their synagogue; they therefore declared, "He loves our nation" (7:5). The word translated here as "loves" is *agapao*, a Greek word used for the highest and noblest love.

3. The centurion's humility was amazing. People who truly belong to God's kingdom can sense their spiritual bankruptcy. Such was the case with this man. The elders were going to take Jesus to the centurion's house. But the

centurion sent friends to say to Jesus, "Lord, do not trouble yourself, for I am not worthy to have you to come under my roof" (7:6).

4. The centurion's faith was amazing. He told Jesus, "I did not presume to come to you. But say the word, and let my servant be healed" (Luke 7:7). He understood the divine power and authority of Jesus. He realized that Jesus had only to speak the word, and the healing would be accomplished.

This man had amazing love, generosity, mercy, humility, and devotion to God. He had faith that amazed Jesus: "When Jesus heard these things, he marveled at him"; and Jesus said to the multitude, "I tell you, not even in Israel have I found such faith" (7:9).

What was wrong with Israel? They were blind in their self-righteousness.

Then came the miracle: "And when those who had been sent returned to the house, they found the servant well" (7:10). Unfathomable! Jesus never touched the servant. He never laid eyes on the servant. This long-distance healing had nothing to do with the servant's faith, for we aren't told whether the servant had faith. The compassionate miracle of Jesus had everything to do with the faithful intercession of one who considered himself unworthy to come into the presence of Jesus. He simply believed that all Jesus had to do was to say the word.

This centurion was a living illustration of the sermon Jesus had preached shortly before entering Capernaum.

Many of the attributes Jesus talked about were true of this man.

Let's pray for an amazing faith to be alive in us as well.

Questions for Reflection

1. What do we learn from the way the centurion approached Jesus?

2. What's the significance of the centurion's "Just say the word" comment?

8

Miracle: Jesus Heals a Paralytic

Read Matthew 9:1-8; Mark 2:1-12; Luke 5:17-26

I have a friend who looks for every opportunity to tell others about Jesus. I'm not exaggerating when I say *every* opportunity. He's the most dedicated and gifted conversational evangelist I've ever met. From restaurants in the US to barrios in Nicaragua, I've watched my friend make new acquaintances. I'm always amazed at how quickly he gracefully moves the conversation to spiritual matters. He has a passion for getting people to Jesus.

In Mark 2, we find a story about four men who went to extreme measures to get a friend to Jesus. They literally ripped off a roof to get this man into the presence of Jesus. The man was paralyzed, and there was no known cure for his condition. These men had heard about Jesus, or maybe even witnessed Him heal others. They realized He was the only remedy for their friend's great need. Their desperation birthed a strong determination.

Jesus was in a house preaching the Word of God, and "many were gathered together so that there was no more room, not even at the door" (2:2). These four men, carrying their paralyzed friend on a mat, didn't let the crowdedness

44

prevent them from getting to Jesus. "And when they could not get near him because of the crowd, they removed the roof above him, and when they had made an opening, they let down the bed on which the paralytic lay" (2:4).

These guys were determined to overcome the obstacles between them and Jesus.

The first obstacle was the crowd. The world wants to keep us from getting to Jesus. Our lives can easily become full of things that take up time, attention, and resources that should be given to the Lord.

The men also rose above barriers. Are you willing to go around the crowd, rise above barriers, and break through obstacles to lay your burdens at the feet of Jesus?

Though I hate to admit this, I often fail in my efforts to intercede for others. I'm not always deeply moved by people's needs. How about you? Are you desperate to help people to Jesus? Are you willing to overcome difficult obstacles to intercede for them?

Intertwined with this remarkable miracle is what Jesus communicated beyond His compassion for one who was broken physically. We read that when Jesus saw the faith of this man's friends, He said to the paralytic, "Son, your sins are forgiven" (2:5). The scribes considered these words to be blasphemy, because only God can forgive sins. Jesus, knowing these thoughts, responded this way:

"But that you may know that the Son of Man has authority on earth to forgive sins"—he said to the paralytic— "I say to you, rise, pick up your bed, and go home." And he rose and immediately picked up his bed and went out before them all, so that they were all amazed and glorified God, saying, "We never saw anything like this!" (2:10-12)

The message to the scribes was that Jesus has the power to heal not only physically but also spiritually. Jesus wanted everyone to know He has the authority to forgive sin. This was unfathomable. The scribes, and everyone looking on, were to conclude that Jesus is God—a response that can be accepted only by faith.

Questions for Reflection

1. Why did Jesus say "your sins are forgiven" instead of telling the young man to "get up and walk"?

2. Which is most important: "Get up and walk" or "Your sins are forgiven"?

3. Do you see needs in others that only Jesus can meet?

9

Miracle: Jesus Heals a Withered Hand

Read Matthew 12:9-14; Mark 3:1-6; Luke 6:6-11

I lost vision in my right eye when I was a baby because an infection left scar tissue over my cornea. I didn't lose the eye itself, but the blindness resulted in the muscles around my eye becoming lazy over time from lack of use. The term used to describe this type of weakness is atrophy.

In this miracle we look at next, Jesus demonstrated that He's the answer for both physical and spiritual atrophy.

When Jesus entered the synagogue, the Pharisees watched Him closely. Having heard stories about the miracles and growing popularity of Jesus, these so-called religious leaders were becoming concerned about the man from Galilee who constantly violated the Sabbath. They were angry that Jesus claimed to forgive men's sins, ate meals with sinners, and refused to honor their rituals.

Just prior to the events described in Matthew 12:9-14, Jesus allowed His disciples to pick and eat grain on the Sabbath (12:1-8). After reminding the Pharisees of past situations that illustrated how the law was meant to serve man rather than man serving the law, Jesus said, "For the Son of Man is lord of the Sabbath" (12:8).

With every miracle and every message, Jesus revealed the intentions of God's heart. In doing so, He exposed the wrong understanding and misapplication of God's law by the Jewish religious establishment. And they despised Him for it.

Jesus entered the synagogue, "and a man was there with a withered hand" (12:10). Some translations describe the man's hand as "paralyzed." The man probably kept his hand out of sight as much as possible. The Pharisees noticed this man in the crowd—or perhaps they'd intentionally arranged for him to be there. Then they watched Jesus to see what He would do.

Jesus responded with a penetrating question: "Which of you who has a sheep, if it falls into a pit on the Sabbath, will not take hold of it and lift it out?" (12:11). The Pharisees had no answer for Jesus, because any honest response they might have given would have contradicted their own teachings. Jesus then drove home His point: "Of how much more value is a man than a sheep! So it is lawful to do good on the Sabbath" (12:12).

These religious leaders weren't concerned about the needs of a poor injured man. They cared only about their rules and their positions of authority. Mark tells us that they suffered from hardness of heart (Mark 3:5); the Greek word translated as "hardness" is used to describe a type of marble, and it eventually came to be used of something covered with a callus. A callous heart is insensitive to the voice of the Lord.

In spite of the Pharisees' attempt to trap Him, Jesus had the man stretch out his hand. When he did, the hand was healed! Jesus's anger at the hypocrisy of those who were supposed to minister compassion didn't prevent him from healing the injured man.

Each of us attempts to cover up the parts of us that are spiritually withered. Is there an aspect of your life that could be described as paralyzed, atrophied, or wasted away? Perhaps it's a damaged relationship, or a neglected prayer life. Maybe you feel paralyzed financially, or your marriage has become lifeless and unhappy.

Jesus stands ready to restore life to what has become dead. Stretch out that which has withered in your life, and ask Jesus to restore life to it.

Questions for Reflection

1. Why did Jesus ask the Pharisees about lifting a sheep out of a pit on the Sabbath?

2. Jesus was both angered and grieved at their hardness of heart (Mark 3:5). What does that mean to you personally?

3. What did Jesus mean when He said, "The Son of Man is Lord of the Sabbath"?

1 0

Miracle: Jesus Raises a Widow's Son

Read Luke 7:11-17

Two processions of people converged outside the gates of the town of Nain. In one group, the central figure was a corpse. In the other, it was Christ. In one procession, there was great sadness and sorrow. In the other, there was joy and gladness. As these two groups converged, life met death.

In Luke 7 we read, "As He drew near to the gate of the town, behold, a man who had died was being carried out, the only son of his mother, and she was a widow, and a considerable crowd from the town was with her" (7:12).

We know only a little about this mother. She was a widow, she'd lost her only son, she lived in Nain, and she had some friends. Was she wealthy? Was she a good person? Did she know Jesus? Was she a person of faith? Was there something about her that made her a candidate for what Jesus was about to do? Scripture doesn't reveal those things to us. But Jesus heard her cry and had compassion on her: "And when the Lord saw her, he had compassion on her and said to her, 'Do not weep'" (7:13).

Why did Jesus perform this particular miracle for these particular people in this particular way? I believe we can discover the answer by considering this biblical truth: Jesus came in the flesh to reveal God's plan to resurrect those who are spiritually dead to new life. While Jesus walked the earth, He displayed God's glory.

Jesus's compassion for this mother wasn't attached to any merit on her part. He was not rewarding her for living a good life. He simply responded to her pain as an act of grace and mercy.

Aren't you glad that we have a great High Priest at the right hand of the Father who can sympathize with our pain and suffering (Hebrews 4:15)?

The Bible is full of promises (such as those in Psalms 34:17 and 55:16) that assure us that God hears the cries of His people. As far as we know, this woman wasn't a believer. Yet Jesus heard her cry, felt her grief, and responded. Once more we see the truth of what Isaiah prophesied: "A bruised reed he will not break, and a smoldering wick he will not quench" (Isaiah 42:3; quoted in Matthew 12:20).

Jesus demonstrates compassion for all who face spiritual death. His plan to save those who respond in faith is a result of His sovereign grace, not our personal merit.

This young man wasn't permanently resurrected that day by Jesus; he would once again die a physical death at some point in the future. But through him, Jesus demonstrated His power to resurrect the dead.

This story is a picture of what Jesus does for those who are dead in sin. He comes in grace (Ephesians 2:8-9) and offers compassion, even though we don't deserve Him. He wants to delivers us from our hopeless condition and to bring us out of death into life (John 5:24; Ephesians 2:1-5). Therefore we can now confidently await our own resurrection into eternal life.

What Jesus did that day in Nain, He did in my life. I couldn't get to God, but He came to me. While I was dead in my sins, He heard my cry and came to me with grace. He gave me life eternal.

What Jesus did that day in Nain, He desires to do in everyone's life who comes to him in repentant humble faith. What a Savior! Unfathomable!

Questions for Reflection

1. What significance is there in the statement that the dead man was "the only son of his mother"?

2. How did the people respond to the powerful presence of God?

11

Miracle: Jesus Calms the Storm

Read Matthew 8:23-27; Mark 4:35-41; Luke 8:22-25

Did you know that in each twenty-four period, a giraffe needs only between twenty minutes and two hours of sleep? Imagine all you could accomplish if you needed only two hours of sleep each night.

The science of sleep is a fascinating subject. Researchers have offered many theories to explain why we need sleep, but they haven't answered the question definitively. Humans have a circadian rhythm of approximately twenty-four hours. During sleep time, several internal systems reset—according to "Brain Basics" information at the website of the National Institute of Neurological Disorders and Strokes:

Sleep affects almost every type of tissue and system in the body—from the brain, heart, and lungs to metabolism, immune function, mood, and disease resistance. Research shows that a chronic lack of sleep, or getting poor quality sleep, increases the risk of disorders including high blood pressure, cardiovascular disease, diabetes, depression, and obesity. Sleep is a complex and dynamic process that affects how you function in ways scientists are now beginning to understand. ("Brain Basics: Understanding Sleep" https://www.ninds.nih.gov/Disorders/Patient-Caregiver-Education/Understanding-Sleep)

The human body requires sleep—but what about God? Does He sleep?

Scripture tells us that God neither sleeps nor slumbers (Psalm 121:4). But Jesus, the Son of God, slept. He even slept through a storm. Let's see what we can learn from the story of Jesus being roused from a nap to calm a furious storm on the sea.

One day Jesus instructed His disciples to get into a boat and go to the other side of the lake. Along the way, a great storm arose. The King James translation describes the storm as a great tempest. The Greek word Matthew used to describe the storm is *seismos* (Matthew 8:24), from which we get the word *seismic.* This was a violent storm. Waves broke over the sides of the boat, filling it with water. The disciples, some of whom were fishermen and had been on this lake many times, were scared. Yet in the middle of the commotion, Jesus was sleeping on a cushion in the back of the boat.

The disciples woke Him and said, "Teacher! Don't you care that we're going to die?" (Mark 4:38). Their fear of perishing was greater than their confidence in the presence of Jesus.

Can you relate to the feeling of desperation the disciples experienced? Maybe you've wondered whether God is aware of what's happening in your life. Well, the details in this story can give us a proper perspective.

Consider what Jesus encountered just prior to this event. His family, thinking He was crazy, had tried to take Him home (Mark 3:21). The Pharisees accused Him of being possessed by the prince of demons (3:22). Jesus had been teaching in parables that His listeners didn't understand. And He healed the sick wherever He went. In the flesh, He had every reason to be exhausted.

The Lord heard His men's desperate cries. He got up and rebuked the wind, then said to the sea, "Peace, be still." No theatrics. Jesus spoke to the wind, and the wind stopped instantaneously; He spoke to the water, and the waves stopped instantaneously. The water and the wind recognized the voice of their Creator.

Just as Jesus would later tell death to release Lazarus, He told the wind and the waves to obey His will. Both the wind and waves ceased, and "there was a great calm" —a phrase stressing the intensity of the calmness. The violent storm was instantly replaced by an extraordinary calm. This is the degree of calmness the Lord can bring to bear on our circumstances.

At the same time that the transition from storm to calm occurred, another transition was taking place. The disciples moved from a great fear of the storm to another type of fear. The fear of the storm was replaced with a reverent awe of Jesus: "And they were filled with great fear and said to one another, 'Who then is this, that even the wind and the sea obey him?'" (Mark 4:41)

Who is this? That's a question we all must answer. In John 1:1-3, we read that Jesus was with God in the beginning, and that through Him all things were created. Jesus took on flesh and lived among us (1:14).

The apostle Paul speaks of this reality about Jesus in this way:

> He is the image of the invisible God, the firstborn over all creation. For everything was created by Him, in heaven and on earth, the visible and the invisible, whether thrones or dominions or rulers or authorities— all things have been created through Him and for Him. He is before all things, and by Him all things hold together. (Colossians 1:15-17)

And the author of the book Hebrews writes this:

The Son is the radiance of God's glory and the exact expression of His nature, sustaining all things by His powerful word. After making purification for sins, He sat down at the right hand of the Majesty on high. (Hebrews 1:3)

God the Son took on a human body, yet remained fully God. His two natures—human and divine—are inseparable. And Jesus sustains all things by His word.

Even while Jesus was sleeping in the back of that boat, He was sustaining the world that He created. He may have been asleep in the flesh, but He was wide awake in His divine nature.

Jesus preserved the disciples in the boat with Him, as well as those who accompanied them in the other boats (Mark 4:36). When Jesus had said, "Let us cross over to the other side" (4:35), it was both a command and a promise.

God never sleeps, and He'll fulfill His promises to all those in His fleet—to get them to the other side.

As Christians, we must answer the question posed by the disciples: "Who then is this that even the wind and the sea obey him?" Jesus stands before us and fills us with reverent awe, with what the Old Testament writers call the fear of the Lord. But this fear—this terrible and beautiful awe—is not at all like that terror brought on by the chaotic storms of this world. No, this is the unfathomable and wondrous creator God, who keeps us afloat in the violent storms of life. And His question to us is: *Why are you afraid?*

Questions for Reflection

1. How does Jesus's calming of the storm differ from His casting out a demon?

2. The disciples were right to turn to Jesus, yet Jesus responded by saying, "Have you still no faith?" What did He mean by this?

1 2

Miracle: Jesus Casts Demons into a Herd of Pigs

Read Matthew 8:28-33; Mark 5:1-20; Luke 8:26-39

Jesus once encountered two men who lived among tombs, and one of the men spoke to Jesus (as we see in Matthew 8:28). The man who spoke is described as having an unclean spirit, and he was always crying out and cutting himself. He wore no clothes and didn't live in a house. Efforts to bind him were fruitless because he was strong enough to break chains. No one could subdue him.

The demons who possessed the man acknowledged Jesus's authority over them by causing the man to fall before Jesus and beg not to be tormented by Him. The demons also "begged him not to command them to depart into the abyss" (Luke 8:31).

The demon within the man identified itself as "Legion, for we are many" (Mark 5:9). When Jesus commanded the legion of demons to come out of the man, they asked to be sent into a nearby herd of pigs.

Why? Even though I enjoy bacon and barbecued pork, I have to admit that pigs are nasty animals. Years ago I helped chase down a pig at a farm in Nicaragua. The pig was being donated to a hungry family living in the barrios. The pig pen was filthy, and the slop the pigs ate smelled horrible. I certainly wouldn't want to live the life of a pig.

Apparently the demons preferred pig-life to the abyss. Their request may have been an effort to avoid being sent early to the place of punishment.

Jesus said that Satan "was a murderer from the beginning and has not stood in the truth, because there is no truth in him. When he tells a lie, he speaks from his own nature, because he is a liar and the father of liars" (John 8:44).

Satan's strategy is to deceitfully imitate God, pervert His Word, tempt mankind, and hinder the work and prayers of His people.

The demons had caused this man to be driven away from the living to dwell among the dead. He was robbed of family and friends. He had no job, and he ran around naked. He'd lost his dignity. No one could help him. His situation appeared hopeless.

But an encounter with Jesus changed everything for him. At the end of this story, the man was dressed and in his right mind. Jesus did more than bring hope. He brought a new reality.

Jesus is the God of reversal, revision, restoration, and redemption. He can demolish even the best efforts of the enemy. He has the power to set people free from bondage and the grip of sin.

The possessed man was able to break physical chains— but only Jesus could break the man's spiritual bondage.

Questions for Reflection

1. The pigs numbered about two thousand (Mark 5:13). Do you think this had anything to do with the people asking Jesus to leave?

2. How did the man from whom the demons had gone respond to what Jesus did for him?

3. What had the demons taken from the man?

1 3

Miracle: Jesus Heals a Woman in the Crowd

Read Matthew 9:20-22; Mark 5:25-34; Luke 8:42-48

Imagine suffering with chronic bleeding every day for twelve years. Consider the sanitary challenges, as well as the health issues resulting from being weak and anemic. Not to mention the embarrassment.

Now picture having those problems in biblical times, without the advances of modern medicine. And in a time when such an ailment meant being cut off from family and friends because you were considered unclean.

Desperate for a cure, you've spent everything you had on doctors. Under their care, your condition has only worsened.

The woman described in Mark 5:25-34 was in terrible misery. She was out of options and had no hope—until she heard about a Jewish carpenter going around teaching, preaching, and performing miracles of healing. Hearing so many stories about Him, she came to believe that if she could somehow get to Jesus and touch Him, she would be healed.

This frail, sickly woman learned that Jesus was coming to her village. Somehow she managed to fight through the crowd surrounding Him and come up behind Him. She didn't speak to Jesus, because she was ashamed of her illness. She wanted to avoid exposure and the humiliating treatment she would receive from people if they noticed her. She would just touch Him quickly, receive her healing, then slip away unnoticed.

When she touched the hem of His garment, she was immediately healed. And in that instant Jesus knew what had happened. He turned around and acknowledged her, right in front of everyone.

Jesus didn't want to embarrass her. He wanted her to acknowledge what had occurred, as a witness to others.

Jesus looked at the woman and said, "Daughter, your faith has made you well" (Luke 8:48). The word translated here as "daughter" is a term of affectionate endearment. Jesus then said, "Go in peace"—or literally, "Go *into* peace," meaning, "Go from this place and walk in good health; you are healed physically and spiritually."

In the middle of that crowd pressing in on all sides, Jesus had felt the weak and desperate hand of faith, and He stopped. He was not too busy to bother with her. He spoke to her as if she were the only person around.

Have you ever felt lost in the crowd? Have you ever struggled with feelings of insignificance? *Do I really matter to God?*

God knows you and loves you as if you were the only person in the universe. Unfathomable, but true! He knows when you reach out to Him in desperation. Whatever it is that hurts you, He feels it. He steps into your pain and suffering.

That's what the writer to the Hebrews meant when he said, "We do not have a high priest who is unable to sympathize with our weaknesses" (Hebrews 4:15).

Whatever hurts us also hurts Him.

Questions for Reflection

1. What is represented by the woman's touching of "the fringe of his garment"?

2. Why did the woman attempt to touch Jesus without being noticed?

14

Miracle: Jesus Raises Jairus's Daughter to Life

Read Matthew 9:18,23-26; Mark 5:21-24; 5:35-43; Luke 8:40-42; 8:49-56

As ruler of the local synagogue, the man named Jairus had prestige, power, and position. And yet he loved his daughter enough to risk it all.

Most of Jairus's peers had an unfavorable opinion of Jesus. They claimed that He performed miracles by the powers of Satan. In spite of their views, when this man's little girl became deathly ill, Jairus humbly fell at the feet of Jesus, pleading with Him to come and lay hands on her.

Jesus agreed to do so. But on the way to Jairus's home, another person who needed a miracle interrupted them—the woman with the issue of blood, whom we read about in the previous chapter. While Jesus attended to her need, Jairus received a message: "Your daughter is dead; do not trouble the Teacher anymore" (Luke 8:49). The messenger assumed that death had put the daughter beyond the Teacher's power to heal. There was no more need to trouble Him.

Can you imagine Jairus's despair when he received such devastating news? All hope seemed lost. Yet Jesus told Jairus, "Do not be fear; only believe, and she will be well" (Luke 8:50).

Jairus believed, and took Jesus to his home. After Jesus commanded the mourners to leave, He gathered Jairus, Jairus's wife, and three disciples in a room with the daughter. Jesus commanded the little girl to get up—and she rose and began to walk.

Jairus allowed the word of Jesus to be the authority in his home.

Let your children see that you're not ashamed to go to Jesus with your needs. Show them that you have faith in the One you go to church to worship. Seek out Jesus for your family.

And pray for God to move in the hearts of other fathers. The lack of involved dads in our society is a crisis that continues to have devastating consequences.

Questions for Reflection

1. How would you have responded to the interruption of your miracle, had you been in Jairus's position?

2. Has a personal faith response placed your position or prestige at risk?

15

Miracle: Jesus Heals Two Blind Men

Read Matthew 9:27-31

In January 2015, a seventeen-year-old in Palm Beach, Florida impersonated an anesthesiologist. For nearly a month he walked around a hospital wearing a white jacket and carrying a stethoscope. He went into examining rooms and observed other doctors examine patients. Fortunately, he didn't attempt to treat anyone.

In May 2015, a man in Atlanta, Georgia was charged with impersonating an eye doctor for nearly six years. In addition to performing eye examinations, he prescribed medications.

During the past few years, several people have posed as plastic surgeons and performed liposuction and other procedures on patients.

Imagine trusting someone with no medical training to diagnose your health problems and prescribe treatment. Trusting an impostor with your life is a scary thought. Keep that in mind as we examine a miracle of Jesus described in Matthew 9:27-31.

Jesus had departed from the house where He'd raised Jairus's daughter from the dead. As the crowd moved along, two blind men cried out, "Son of David, have mercy on us" (9:27).

This raises an interesting question. Jesus had stopped for the woman with chronic bleeding, and He had stopped to hear Jairus plead for his dying daughter—but He didn't stop for the two blind men. Instead He went on until He came to a house, which He entered. The blind men followed Him inside.

Why didn't Jesus stop and attend to these men while still outside?

After these men expressed faith in Jesus's ability to heal them, Jesus restored their sight. He performed this miracle in the privacy of a home. The Lord then "sternly warned them" in these words: "See that no one knows about it" (9:30). Why this warning? When these guys went back home, their families and friends were going to notice the change. People were going to talk! Hiding this miracle would be impossible.

Why did Jesus warn them not to tell? I think we find the answer in the words the men first spoke: "Have mercy on us, Son of David." The phrase *Son of David* is a statement identifying Jesus as the prophesied Messiah (the Anointed One). Ironically, these men who were physically blind had been granted spiritual insight that even the learned religious leaders did not possess. The Jews were looking for the prophet that Moses foretold and who would come from the line of David.

At this point in His ministry, Jesus wasn't making verbal public claims about being the Messiah. He wasn't presenting Himself as the King of kings. He was on a mission to secure salvation for lost sinners, which meant He was the suffering servant who was destined for the cross. Just as Jesus told a demon to "be silent and come out of him" when the demon identified Jesus as "the Holy One of God" (Luke 4:34-35), so also Jesus didn't entrust these two men to go forth proclaiming Him as the Messiah.

Instead, Jesus let His works be His witness.

Do you remember when John the Baptist asked Jesus if He was the one who was to come? Jesus replied,

> Go and tell John what you hear and see: the blind receive their sight and the lame walk, lepers are cleansed and the deaf hear, and the dead are raised up, and the poor have good news preached to them. (Matthew 11:4-5)

We never have to wonder if Jesus is an impostor. He came and performed the works prophesied of Him long in advance. His works verify His credibility and authenticity. We can trust every promise He has made, because He is who He claims to be.

Questions for Reflection

1. After Jesus warned the healed blind men not tell anyone, "They went away and spread His fame through all that district" (Matthew 9:31). Why did they tell people?

2. When Jesus touched their eyes, He said, "According to your faith be it done to you" (Matthew 9:29). Why did Jesus use that wording?

16

Two Miracles:
Jesus Heals Mute and Blind Demoniacs

Read Matthew 9:32-34; 12:22-23; Luke 11:14-23

Over the years, many concerned Christians have expressed to me their fear that they may have committed an unpardonable sin. Some believers are sincerely concerned that the sum of their sins, or one particular sin, has placed them beyond the possibility of forgiveness by Jesus.

Is that possible? Is there a sin or a degree of sin that the blood of Jesus is not sufficient to cover?

Part of the confusion regarding this issue is due to the wide variety of interpretations of passages that address the unpardonable sin.

Interestingly, it's Jesus who said that there's an unpardonable sin. Against a backdrop of freeing a man from demon possession and healing physical infirmities, Jesus was accused by the Pharisees of driving out demons by the power of Beelzebul, or the prince of demons (Mark 3:22; Matthew 9:34: 12:24). When the Pharisees first made this accusation early in His ministry, Jesus ignored them (Matthew 9:32-34). As opposition from the Pharisees grew, the confrontations became more intense. Finally, after once again being accused of casting out demons by the power of Beelzebul, Jesus offered an irrefutable argument (Matthew 12:25-37) that demonstrated the ridiculousness of their accusation. The central point of Jesus's rebuttal was this: "If Satan casts out Satan, he is divided against himself. How then will his kingdom stand?" (12:26).

In Mark 3:29, Jesus described blasphemy against the Holy Spirit as "an eternal sin," meaning a sin God will not forgive. Maybe the Pharisees had committed this unforgivable sin, or maybe not. But Jesus explained it straightforwardly:

> Therefore I tell you, every sin and blasphemy will be forgiven people, but the blasphemy against the Spirit will not be forgiven. And whoever speaks a word against the Son of Man will be forgiven, but whoever speaks against the Holy Spirit will not be forgiven, either in this age or in the age to come. (Matthew 12:31-34)

When the Pharisees saw the work of the Holy Spirit and called it the work of Satan, they were at least approaching the brink of never-ending guilt. Jesus said that whoever speaks a word against Him will be forgiven, but whoever speaks against the Holy Spirit will not be forgiven. Was Jesus elevating the Holy Spirit above Himself? No, Jesus was actually referring to the ministry of the Spirit. The Holy Spirit draws people to God. There's a point where hardness of heart will place a person beyond the ability to repent. The gospel is clear: Unless there's acceptance of Jesus as Lord and repentance from sin, there's no forgiveness. The Pharisees were in danger of finding themselves beyond repentance.

The unpardonable sin is a denial of the Spirit's message and a rejection of the Lord's deity. Jesus made it clear that adultery, murder, blasphemy, and other sins can be forgiven; they are not unpardonable. The sin that God won't forgive is the rejection of His Son.

Sometimes people wonder if they've committed "the sin against the Holy Spirit." The Holy Spirit bears witness to Christ and convicts the lost sinner. A wise person once said, "If you're honestly worried about whether you've committed it, then you haven't." He meant that such concern is evidence of the Spirit's present work of conviction in a heart, and therefore evidence that the heart isn't irreversibly hardened.

Questions for Reflection

1. The people asked, "Can this be the Son of David?" What did they expect the Son of David to be and do?

2. What did Jesus say about battling Satan's kingdom and the danger of neutrality?

1 7

Miracle: Jesus Heals an Invalid at Bethesda

Read John 5:1-15

One day while Jesus was in Jerusalem for one of the Jewish feasts, He took a trip to a local pool. Normally when we think of a pool, we think of recreational swimming in cool refreshing water. The pool called Bethesda wasn't that kind of pool. Bethesda means "house of mercy," but it might have been more aptly described as a house of misery. Instead of healthy people wearing swimsuits and catching rays, the people around this pool were physically and spiritually broken. John describes them as "a multitude of sick—blind, lame and paralyzed" (John 5:3). The sick people gathered there were constantly staring at the water because they believed that the first person into the pool when the water was stirred would be healed.

Jesus walked up to one particular man and asked if he wanted to be healed. Now that seems like a callous question, doesn't it? Of course the man wanted to be healed; he'd been an invalid for thirty-eight years, having suffered for almost a full lifetime.

We aren't told how long this man has been visiting the pool, but he must have spent countless hours watching the water. He was fixated on what he believed would provide a cure to his problems. He might be described as being obsessed with the pool. Jesus was trying to get the man to take his focus off the pool. Jesus's question was designed to cause the man to focus instead on Jesus.

When Jesus asked if the man wanted to be healed, the invalid didn't answer directly but instead complained about how no one would help him get into the pool. He was trying to solicit Jesus's help to lower him into the water. We're often like that—trying to get Jesus to help us fulfill our own plans.

Jesus isn't going to follow our plans—we must follow His.

Jesus is ready to visit our own pool of Bethesda, which speaks of our condition of spiritual paralysis when we're stuck looking at an object of false hope. Jesus loves us enough to enter our pain and to heal us. Jesus wants to meet us at our own pool of Bethesda!

What is it you're focused on today? What is your pool? What's the thing on which you're fixated? Do you have a false hope that takes your eyes off the Lord? Are you looking to a relationship, a job, a hobby, or possessions to bring you fulfillment?

Jesus gave the man a threefold command: "Get up, take up your bed, and walk." Jesus may have discerned that the man had the faith to be healed, because the broken man obeyed and was healed.

Jesus extended His mercy to this man by later finding the man in the temple. Perhaps this was because the man, after being healed, was at the temple giving thanks. His vision had moved away from the pool.

Jesus told the man to stop sinning, or else something worse might happen to him. Stop sinning! Sin is a doorway to the enemy. Not only must our focus be upon Jesus, but we must pursue holiness.

Mercy was shown in the house of mercy—but the Jews had become so legalistic that they couldn't see this as a work of God. The Jews' fixation on the law prevented them from accepting this miracle of Jesus because it had occurred on the Sabbath. The letter of the law had killed their view of Jesus, the very embodiment of the law.

Are you stuck at your own pool of Bethesda? Jesus was there, but the sick man didn't recognize Him.

While we're focusing on our own pools, Jesus is right next to us. He wants to move us away from attempting to fulfill our own visions, and instead accept the plans He has for us. Jesus wants to heal us and take our eyes off our own disappointing, insufficient, and powerless pools that lead to nothing but more emptiness.

Questions for Reflection

1. When the Jews saw the healed man carry his bed, onlookers rebuked the man and said, "It's the Sabbath, and

it's not lawful to carry your bed." What are some ways Christians today allow legalism to preclude love?

2. What does "Sin no more" imply about the man's physical suffering?

1 8

Miracle: Jesus Feeds Five Thousand

Read Matthew 14:13-21; Mark 6:30-44; Luke 9:10-17; John 6:1-15

The story of Jesus feeding the five thousand begins on a somber note. Prior to telling this story, the Gospels report the beheading of John the Baptist.

Not only were the disciples heartbroken over John's death, but Mark and Luke explain that Jesus had recently sent twelve disciples out to preach repentance, and on their return, Jesus sought to get the disciples away for some much needed rest (Mark 6:31). But the planned recuperation had to wait, because the crowds saw them leaving and followed. In spite of the circumstances, Mark reports Jesus teaching the people. Matthew adds that Jesus healed those who were sick. Jesus's compassion eventually led to a discussion about feeding the multitude.

He asked Philip, "Where are we to buy bread that these people may eat?" (John 6:5). Philip responded that a hundred denarii wouldn't be enough money to buy enough bread so that each person could have even a small bite.

Jesus said, "How many loaves do you have? Go and see" (Mark 6:38). In other words, take an inventory.

The disciple Andrew pointed out a small boy who had two fish and five barley loaves. Andrew added, "But what are they for so many?" (John 6:8-9). If I'd been there, I would have agreed with Andrew. Five loaves and two fish were utterly insufficient to feed five thousand.

That is—until you put them into the hands of Jesus. When heaven's math kicks in, five loaves plus two fish equals five thousand. And let's not forget the twelve baskets of leftovers.

The place where Jesus was teaching the people is described as being "desolate" (Matthew 14:13,15). There Jesus not only healed the sick but also gave everyone food: "And they all ate and were satisfied" (Mark 6:42).We have a Savior who meets our needs in desolate places where our strength and resources are at an end.

When the disciples had told Jesus about the two fish and five loaves, Jesus had said, "Bring them here to me" (Matthew 14:18). Jesus prayed, broke the bread and fish into pieces, and fed five thousand men plus women and children.

(Was there something special about the number of loaves and fish? Apparently not. When Jesus later fed the four thousand, we read in Matthew 15:34 that IIe used seven loaves "and a few small fish.")

Why didn't Jesus feed the crowd in some other way? Why not a different menu? Couldn't He have caused manna to fall from heaven? Couldn't He have caused steak and potatoes to appear out of nowhere? Maybe throw in a salad? Sure, He could have. Instead He decided to have them take inventory of what they had available. Why? Because God desires for us to give Him what we have as an expression of faith. He involves us in His work.

God works with what we have. In the story of Elijah and the widow, He used flour and oil. Moses gave God his staff. God used David's sling to slay a giant.

Are you struggling in an area of your life because you're lacking provision? Take inventory, and place what you have in God's hands.

Questions for Reflection

1. Mark describes the crowd as "like sheep without a shepherd." What's the significance of that description? What does it means to you?

2. After this miracle, Jesus perceived that people wanted to take Him by force and make Him king, so He withdrew to a mountain by Himself (John 6:15). What was the misunderstanding the people had about His kingship?

19

Miracle: Jesus Walks on Water

Read Matthew 14:22-33; Mark 6:45-52; John 6:16-21

The story of Jesus walking on water—in the midst of a storm, in the wee hours of the morning—is one of my favorites. This story is rich in spiritual truth, but I want to zero in on one question: Why did Jesus get in the boat?

In the early evening, after feeding a crowd of more than five thousand, Jesus sent the disciples on ahead of Him. "Immediately he made his disciples get into the boat and go before him to the other side, to Bethsaida, while he dismissed the crowd" (Mark 6:45). That night, a storm arose—and though the disciples had been straining against the oars all night long, they'd progressed only three or four miles. They were in the middle of the lake when Jesus came walking up.

Mark describes the scene as if Jesus was about to pass them by when the frightened disciples cried out (Mark 6:48)—at which point Jesus responded, "Take heart; it is I. Do not be afraid." Matthew describes Peter's incredible steps of faith and his subsequent faltering when he saw the wind and the waves. After that, Jesus and Peter got into the boat, and the sea and the wind grew calm. "And when they got into the boat, the wind ceased. And those in the boat worshiped him, saying, 'Truly you are the Son of God'" (Matthew 14:32-33). Unfathomable!

The apostle John writes, "Then they were glad to take him into the boat, and immediately the boat was at the land to which they were going" (John 6:21). In an instant they were moved from the middle of the lake to the shore.

Back to the question I posed in the beginning. Why did Jesus get in the boat? He could have continued walking on the water all the way to the other shore, or He could have transported Himself—and the boat full of disciples—to the shore without getting in the boat.

Keep in mind that the reason the disciples were in the boat to begin with is that Jesus told them to get into it and go to the other side. In other words, they were exactly where Jesus told them to be, and they were attempting to do what He'd commanded them to do.

Think of the boat as a picture of the church, and think of the disciples as members of the church. In the boat you have tax collectors, betrayers, those who would deny Jesus, and all manner of sinners—you get the picture. So here's the church trying in their own strength to do what Jesus commanded, and making little headway. Jesus steps into the boat in response to their fearful cries, and everything changes. They experience His presence, and they worship. The sea and wind grow calm, and suddenly supernatural things are occurring.

I believe Jesus stepped into the boat to communicate His desire to be with them—and to say to them, "I can give you strength to do the things I've called you to do. Even in the darkest of nights and the deepest of storms, I'll come to you. If you want to battle in your own strength, I'll let you; however, if you'll call to me in faith, then I'll bring you through, and you'll experience Me in a profound way."

Are you in a storm today? Is your boat taking on water? Are you making little headway? Are you battling in your own strength? Invite Jesus into your boat.

Many years ago I took private pilot lessons. My instructor drilled into my head what I was to do if I ever found myself spiraling out of control in a spin. He said, "If you ever find yourself in a spin, let go of the steering and rudder. The plane will straighten." As you've probably guessed, one afternoon I was practicing stalls and I ended up in a spin. I tried to correct with the stick and rudder, but nothing happened. I desperately tried to make the needed corrections. Finally, with the ground quickly approaching, I did what my instructor said. I let go. When I took my hands off the controls, the plane immediately came out of the spin. In my own struggle to control the plane, I intensified the conditions that caused the plane to spin in the first place.

I know it's a cliché, but sometimes we just need to let go and let God.

Questions for Reflection

1. How did Jesus respond to the disciples' fearfulness?

2. Mark includes this information in the story: "And he got into the boat with them, and the wind ceased. And they were utterly astounded, for they did not understand about the loaves, but their hearts were hardened" (Mark 6:51). What did Mark mean by saying their hearts were hardened?

3. Why did Jesus send the disciples ahead without going with them? See Mark 6:46. What does this say to us?

20

Miracle: Jesus Heals a Gentile Woman's Demon-Possessed Daughter

Read Matthew 15:21-28; Mark 7:24-30

I don't think of crumbs in a positive light. After all, they're only tiny pieces of food that tend to end up on the floor. They're swept out with a broom or licked off the floor by a pet. When we have a need in any area of our life, we're likely to be insulted if we're offered only "crumbs" to meet that need—only a fraction of the desired medicine, surgery, repair, resources, friendship, or love. It might as well be nothing at all.

In Matthew 15:21-28 and Mark 7:24-30 we read of a woman with a desperate need the world cannot meet. Her daughter is demon-possessed. The woman is a Greek living in Syrian Phoenicia. Since she's a Gentile, she's considered by Jews to be on the level of a dog. She cannot go to the synagogue and ask the Jewish priest to perform an exorcism. She has nowhere to turn.

Do you relate? Maybe your need is overwhelming and you feel your situation is hopeless. Don't give up hope! As it turns out, the woman's answer was crumbs. Keep reading, and see what happens when this mother approached Jesus.

When the woman heard that Jesus and His disciples had traveled to her region—approximately forty to fifty miles north of the Sea of Galilee—she went to beg for His help. She had quite a few obstacles to overcome. Although she addressed Jesus as the Son of David, "He did not answer her a word" (Matthew 15:23). She'd clearly heard of Jesus and knew about the miracles He'd performed and understood something of the prophesied Jewish Messiah, but being a Gentile, she had no right to approach Jesus on that basis. Not only that, but she was a woman in a culture where women were little respected. The disciples urged Jesus to send her away because she kept crying out.

Finally the woman addressed Jesus as Lord (15:25). His response is one that many of us, in our pride, would view as a huge insult: "It isn't right to take the children's bread and throw it to their dogs" (15:26). Did Jesus insinuate that this woman was a dog? The Greek word used by Jesus refers to a household pet, like a puppy. Notice also that Jesus never said the puppy wouldn't be feed, but that the children would be given bread first. This fits with Jesus being sent first to the lost sheep of Israel.

The woman displayed tremendous humility and life-changing faith. She didn't allow her pride to blind her regarding her need. She fully comprehended her unworthiness before Jesus. "Yes, Lord," she said, "yet even the dogs eat the crumbs that fall from their master's table" (15:27).

Hearing that, Jesus commended the woman for having "great faith," and He healed her daughter (Matthew 15:28). Jesus wasn't trying to be difficult; rather, He was helping the mother display a faith that perseveres.

The world we live in offers a huge and appetizing buffet. The problem is that the world's buffet will leave us starving spiritually. If you're like me, you would rather have crumbs from the Master's table than exquisite delicacies from the world's buffet. The crumbs from the King's table provide nourishment that's both spiritual and eternal.

We're invited to come to Jesus and live. Like this mother, we must come in humility and faith. Don't give up! Keep looking to Jesus in spite of the obstacles in your life. Rejoice to have crumbs from the King's table.

Questions for Reflection

1. How would you have responded to Jesus if he compared you to a dog?

2. The disciples wanted Jesus to send the woman away. What did Jesus teach them by causing the demon to leave the woman's daughter?

3. What did Jesus mean by "the children's bread"?

2 1

Miracle: Jesus Heals a Deaf and Dumb Man

Read Mark 7:31-37

"Friends don't let friends drive drunk"—that familiar slogan has been frequently amended on bumper stickers and t-shirts to communicate various messages. For example: Friends don't let friends do stupid things alone. Friends don't let friends wear bad outfits.

Seriously, a true friend will try to prevent a friend from being hurt. Proverbs 18:24 says that there's a friend who sticks closer than a brother. Ask yourself what kind of friend you are. Are you a really good friend? Do you care about the welfare of your close friends? How much do you care?

In Mark 7:31-37, we meet a man with severe disabilities. He was both deaf and mute. Fortunately, he had friends who were concerned enough about his condition to want to help.

Mark is the only Gospel writer to record this miracle, which occurred in the region of the Decapolis. This area was made up of mostly Gentiles. In this section of Mark's

Gospel we see Jesus ministering to Gentiles and demonstrating His care and concern for all people.

The people in the region had heard of Jesus. This was the same area where Jesus had cast demons out of a man and sent the demons into a herd of pigs. Word about that incident had no doubt gotten around, as well as stories of other miracles Jesus had performed.

The picture Mark gives us in 7:32 is of some people bringing this man to Jesus. Mark refers to these persons only as "they." How often have you ever used the word "they" when telling a story. Perhaps when you've heard others mention "they" without naming anyone, you've wondered who exactly makes up that group.

We don't know the exact identity of "they" in Mark 7:32. Maybe they were friends or family members. What we do know is that they cared enough to get this man to Jesus.

Notice what they did. They begged and pleaded with Jesus. They were desperate to have Him touch this man who had this physical problem. The Greek is specific about the man's speech disability. He had a speech impediment and was also deaf. His physical need was visible. He also had a spiritual need of which they weren't aware.

Let me ask you: Are you begging Jesus on behalf of your friends who have a need? This man obviously had a physical need. We, too, have friends with physical needs. We also have friends with spiritual needs. Are you interceding for these friends? Are you praying for them?

Are you pleading with Jesus on their behalf? Are you trying to get them to Jesus?

Questions for Reflection

1. Why do you think Jesus took the man "aside from the crowd privately"? (Mark 7:33)

2. What was the purpose of Jesus touching the man's ears and tongue as He healed him?

3. We learn from Mark 6:34 that Jesus looked up to heaven and sighed before He commanded the man's ears to be open. Why did Jesus sigh?

22

Miracle: Jesus Feeds Four Thousand

Read Matthew 15:32-39; Mark 8:1-13

On two separate occasions, Jesus fed thousands of people with a handful of fish and loaves. I've always thought of the feeding of the four thousand as a parallel and somewhat secondary miracle to the feeding of the five thousand—almost as if the second was needed to confirm that the first wasn't a fluke.

There are many parallels between these two stories. The most significant parallel may be that Jesus looked at the crowds and had compassion on them. We see this again in the second story:

> In those days, when again a great crowd had gathered, and they had nothing to eat, he called his disciples to him and said to them, "I have compassion on the crowd, because they have been with me now three days and have nothing to eat. And if I send them away hungry to their homes, they will faint on the way. And some of them have come from far away." (Mark 8:1-3)

In both accounts, the disciples asked where enough bread could be found to feed so many. Each meal ended with lots of food left over. Each was also a sign pointing to the deity of Jesus. With both miracles, Jesus used physical realities to demonstrate spiritual truths—and this is where the two miracles take us down different paths.

The feeding of the five thousand (John 6:6-14) had set in motion a series of events that culminated in Capernaum, where Jesus preached the "Bread of Life" sermon (John 6:22-59). Later, in the aftermath of the feeding of the four thousand, Jesus told His disciples to "watch and beware of the leaven of the Pharisees and Sadducees" (Matthew 16:6). Some translations use the word yeast rather than leaven. With the exception of the parable about leaven found in Matthew 13, leaven is used in Scripture to symbolize evil or sin.

In the story of Israel's exodus from Egypt, God commanded His people to prepare unleavened bread and eat it for seven consecutive days (Exodus 12). They were instructed to remove leaven from their houses, and whoever ate leaven was to be cut off from the congregation of Israel (12:19). Refraining from leaven illustrated their separation from the world and a dedication to purity in their relationship to Yahweh.

Leaven or yeast mixes throughout the dough. In the same way, Jesus warned the disciples of the danger of the spreading leaven of the Pharisees and Sadducees. In Matthew 16:12, the disciples finally "understood that he did not tell them to beware of the leaven of bread, but of the teaching of the Pharisees and Sadducees."

Jesus had a lot to say about the hypocritical teaching of the Scribes and Pharisees, as in this quite sobering passage:

> Woe to you, scribes and Pharisees, hypocrites! For you shut the kingdom of heaven in people's faces. For you neither enter yourselves nor allow those who would enter to go in. Woe to you, scribes and Pharisees, hypocrites! For you travel across sea and land to make a single proselyte, and when he becomes a proselyte, you make him twice as much a child of hell as yourselves. (Matthew 23:13-15)

The earlier feeding of the five thousand had led to a conversation about the bread of life leading to eternal life, found only in Jesus. The feeding of the four thousand led to a warning about false teaching and hypocrisy.

Then and now, many people searching for eternal life have found themselves led astray by false teaching. The warning of Jesus is as valid to believers today as it was to believers in His day. Beware the leaven of false teachers. Beware of those who take Scripture out of context. Some call it proof-texting. Always compare what you hear or read to the full counsel of God's Word. Use Scripture to prove Scripture.

Questions for Reflection

1. In the feeding of the five thousand and His subsequent sermon, Jesus communicated to a Jewish crowd

that He was the bread of life. What is the significance of His feeding a crowd of four thousand (mostly Gentiles) in a similar way?

2. The people "ate and were satisfied" (Mark 8:8); what does this tell us about the sufficiency of Jesus's provision?

2 3

Miracle: Jesus Heals a Blind Man at Bethsaida

Read Mark 8:22-26

One day while Jesus was in a town called Bethsaida, a blind man was brought to Him. The people of Bethsaida who brought this man "begged Jesus to touch him" (Mark 8:22). Their motivation wasn't so much an issue of compassion and concern as it was a desire to see Jesus perform another miracle. How ironic. The people leading the physically blind were spiritually blind and didn't know it. Their actions were no more spiritually motivated than when we take a trip to LensCrafters to purchase a new pair of glasses.

The people living in Bethsaida had witnessed many miracles of Jesus, yet they failed to repent and to acknowledge Jesus as the Messiah. As a result, Jesus pronounced future judgment:

> Then he began to denounce the cities where most of his mighty works had been done, because they did not repent. "Woe to you, Chorazin! Woe to you, Bethsaida! For if the mighty works done in you had been done in Tyre and Sidon, they would have repented long ago in sackcloth and ashes. But I tell you, it will be more bearable on the day of judgment for Tyre and Sidon than for you." (Matthew 11:20-22)

Regardless of the wrong motivation of the people, Jesus responded with compassion:

> And he took the blind man by the hand and led him out of the village, and when he had spit on his eyes and laid his hands on him, he asked him, "Do you see anything?" And he looked up and said, "I see people, but they look like trees, walking." Then Jesus laid his hands on his eyes again; and he opened his eyes, his sight was restored, and he saw everything clearly. And he sent him to his home, saying, "Do not even enter the village." (Mark 8:23-26)

Jesus drew this man out of the place of sin. He took the blind man outside the town to heal him. Jesus guided this man to the place where his sight was given. The blind man had to walk with Jesus to get there. I see here a clear illustration of how the Lord leads blind sinners to the place of salvation.

This miracle is unique in that this is the only time in the Gospels where Jesus healed someone in stages. Many times Jesus touched a person or spoke to someone and the healing instantly occurred. This miracle sheds light on the lengthier way that God opens the eyes of the spiritually blind, and it illustrates how God patiently works with those who cannot understand spiritual truth. Step by step, He to moves them to the place of full comprehension.

The timing of this miracle is not a coincidence. In the previous verses, Mark shares a revealing conversation that came about because the disciples had forgotten to bring bread:

> And he cautioned them, saying, "Watch out; beware of the leaven of the Pharisees and the leaven of Herod." And they began discussing with one another the fact that they had no bread. And Jesus, aware of this, said to them, "Why are you discussing the fact that you have no bread? Do you not yet perceive or understand? Are your hearts hardened? Having eyes do you not see, and having ears do you not hear? And do you not remember? When I broke the five loaves for the five thousand, how many baskets full of broken pieces did you take up?" They said to him, "Twelve." "And the seven for the four thousand, how many baskets full of broken pieces did you take up?" And they said to him, "Seven." And he said to them, "Do you not yet understand?" (Mark 8:15-21)

The disciples still lacked a complete understanding of the fullness of Jesus's identity. Jesus questioned their lack of spiritual insight in the face of what they'd witnessed. His mention of eyes that don't see and ears that don't hear might have recalled for them His healing of the deaf and mute man in Mark 7:31-37. The two healings could be seen as symbolic of the spiritual condition of the disciples.

As this later miracle unfolded, Jesus asked the blind man if he could see anything. That same question could be asked of us all.

Do *you* see anything? Is your spiritual sight as keen as it should be? Do you have the Lord in sharp, clear focus in your heart and life? Do you know who He is and understand what He's doing in your life?

Do you see anything?

Have you seen the truth that you stand in need of a Savior? Has the Lord revealed your condition to you? Is He calling you to come to Him? If He is, please don't delay. Come to Jesus while He calls. Come to Jesus now.

Questions for Reflection

1. Why did Jesus lead the man out of town before He healed him?

2. Why did Jesus send the man home and warn him not to go back through the village?

3. What spiritual disciplines might help you *to see more clearly*?

24

Miracle: Jesus Heals a Man Born Blind
(Part One)

Read John 9

The man sat in total darkness. There was light all around, but he couldn't comprehend it.

When Jesus and His disciples came upon this man who was blind from birth, the disciples sought to turn his tragic situation into a theological discussion. They asked, "Rabbi, who sinned, this man or his parents, that he was born blind?" (John 9:2).

Jesus answered that the man's blindness was caused by neither the man's sin nor that of his parents. He then gave the true reason:

> This came about so that God's works might be displayed in him. We must do the works of Him who sent Me while it is day. Night is coming when no one can work. As long as I am in the world, I am the light of the world. (John 9:3-5)

Much more than one man's physical healing occurred in this drama. The Light of the world brought about physical healing to this man's eyes with the gift of physical light, but even more significant was the spiritual dawning of the light of life that Jesus spoke into this man's existence.

John 9 presents an amazing story that we'll examine in two parts. Jesus set the stage for this miracle by declaring Himself "the light of the world" (9:5). Jesus established the context for how we're to examine what took place. If we're to understand this story, we must seek illumination from other Scriptures about darkness and light.

This occasion wasn't the first in which the disciples heard Jesus declare Himself as the light of the world. In fact, almost all of John 8 is about a dispute between Jesus and the Pharisees that started when Jesus declared, "I am the light of the world" (8:12). Light is a symbol used throughout the Bible in connection with Christ. God uses physical light which is real, foundational, and essential to every person as a way to illustrate spiritual truth.

The man blind from birth didn't comprehend physical or spiritual light without the help of Jesus. All men are spiritually blind at birth. No one can comprehend spiritual light without being granted a spiritual birth and spiritual eyes by the Spirit of God. Spiritual sight allows us to see ourselves in light of a holy God. We're sinners who need a Savior. Darkness is not God's plan for us. He sent His Son that we might have light and life.

Later, in explaining why people are condemned who reject the light of Christ, John says this:

> And this is the condemnation, that the light has come into the world, and men loved darkness rather than light, because their deeds were evil. For everyone practicing evil hates the light and does not come to the light, lest his deeds should be exposed. (John 3:19-20)

Note that Jesus wasn't simply saying that He is "a" light to the world, or "another" light to the world. Nor was He saying that He possessed the light, or points out the way to the light. Instead He was declaring that He Himself *is* the one and only light of the world.

The miracle unfolded this way:

> After he said these things he spit on the ground, made some mud from the saliva, and spread the mud on his eyes. "Go," he told him, "wash in the pool of Siloam" (which means "Sent"). So he left, washed, and came back seeing" (John 9:6-7 CSB).

Jesus put spit and dirt in the blind man's eyes! We know that Jesus healed others with just a word or a touch. In fact, Jesus healed some from a distance—as with the Roman centurion's servant, whose physical location was many miles away (Luke 7:1-10).

Here in John 9, why did Jesus use mud? How would you respond if a doctor tried that cure on you? Since saliva was considered medicinal in Jesus's day, maybe saliva was used as a source of encouragement. Most likely the saliva was simply to make the dirt adhere to the man's eyes. Still—how do we explain the use of dirt?

Dirt in the eye is irritating. A minute particle of dust or a tiny eyelash can cause great discomfort in the eye. I suspect the irritating discomfort added to the blind man's motivation to get to the pool to wash his eyes. Later, when asked how his eyes were opened, the blind man responded, "The man called Jesus made mud, spread it on my eyes, and told me, 'Go to Siloam and wash.' So when I went and washed I received my sight" (John 9:11).

All he knew was that a man called Jesus put mud in his eyes and commanded him to go and wash in the pool. Whatever faith the blind man had was aided by the need for relief.

Who would have thought of mud in someone's eye as a beautiful picture of grace? We should be grateful for the irritations Jesus allows in our lives that push us toward faith in the light of the world. Thank the Lord for blessed relief found only in Him, and for washing in the water of His Word.

Questions for Reflection

1. Why might God allow suffering in our lives?

2. Are you willing to suffer that the works of God might be displayed?

25

Miracle: Jesus Heals a Man Born Blind
(Part Two)

Read John 9

In John 9, after rubbing dirt and saliva in the blind man's eyes, Jesus sent the man to the pool of Siloam (9:6-7). John tells us that Siloam means "sent." How the pool earned this name isn't clear. Jesus, who was sent by the Father, sent the blind man to wash in a pool called Sent. The man was healed and quickly became a witness of the power of Christ.

The physical changes in the actions and appearance of this man healed from blindness are undeniable. Neighbors and people who'd seen him before asked each other: Wasn't this the man who used to sit and beg? Some said it was; others said it was only someone like him. But the healed man kept saying, "I am the man" (9:8-9).

The crowd wanted to know how the impossible could have happened. They asked, "Then how were your eyes opened?" (9:10). The blind man's response is almost humorous: "The man called Jesus made mud, and anointed my eyes, and said to me, 'Go to Siloam and wash.' So I went and washed and received my sight" (9:11). The blind man had been unable to see who healed him; all that he knew was that the man was called Jesus.

While the man's physical transformation was undeniable, an unseen spiritual transformation was only just beginning.

Not satisfied with his explanation, some of the people took the man to the Pharisees for questioning. This time when asked about who had healed him, the man responded, "He is a prophet" (9:17).

Still not satisfied, the Pharisees questioned the blind man's parents, who acknowledged their son's previous blindness and his undeniable healing. "How then does he now see?" the Pharisees demanded to know (9:19). The parents responded, "He is of age; ask him" (9:23).

Frustrated, the Pharisees began to insult the man. They claimed to be followers of Moses, who was spoken to by God—they contrasted Moses with Jesus, of whom they said, "As for this man, we don't know where he's from!" (John 9:29 CSB)

The man's response to them is priceless. He became their teacher:

Why, this is an amazing thing. You do not know where he comes from, and yet he opened my eyes. We know that God does not listen to sinners, but if anyone is a worshiper of God and does his will, God listens to him. Never since the world began has it been heard that anyone opened the eye of a man born blind. If this man were not from God, he could do nothing. (John 9:30-34)

The Pharisees called the man a sinner and threw him out. Later, Jesus found the man He'd healed and asked him, "Do you believe in the Son of Man?" (John 9:35). Upon realizing that Jesus is the Son of Man, the man responded, "I believe, Lord," and he worshiped Jesus. The man had received a different kind of healing. He was made alive spiritually.

Notice how the man grew in his faith. He spoke first of "a man they call Jesus." Then he described Jesus as "a prophet." Later he confounded the Pharisees with logic that pointed to Jesus being from heaven. Finally, he confessed Jesus as Lord and worshiped Him. He displayed a beautiful transformation of faith.

The blind man's spiritual transformation would have been as undeniable as his physical healing. The change in his life gave him an opportunity to share his story of Christ's power and compassion. He became a "sent one" by virtue of undeniable change.

We might ask ourselves: Is our spiritual transformation resulting in our being a sent messenger for the Lord?

Questions for Reflection

1. Why did the blind man's parents avoid answering the Pharisees' question?

2. What did Jesus mean when He said to the Pharisees, "If you were blind you would have no guilt; but now that you say, 'We see,' your guilt remains" (John 9:41)?

2 6

Miracle: Jesus Heals a Demon-Possessed Boy

Read Matthew 17:14-20; Mark 9:14-29; Luke 9:37-43

One can only imagine what Peter, James, and John felt as they witnessed the transfiguration of Jesus: "And his clothes became radiant, intensely white, as no one on earth could bleach them. And there appeared to them Elijah with Moses, and they were talking with Jesus" (Mark 9:3-4).

In the afterglow of that supernatural experience, the three disciples and Jesus came down from the mountain to find the other nine disciples surrounded by a crowd and arguing with the teachers of the law (9:14-29).

The issue? A father had sought out Jesus because the father's son was possessed by a demon. The boy was having violent seizures, and sometimes the demon caused the boy to throw himself into fire and water (9:22). When Jesus wasn't available, His disciples attempted an exorcism. Even though Jesus had previously given the disciples authority to cast out demons, and they had successfully done so, this time the disciples couldn't cast out the demon from the boy (Mark 6:7-13). Why?

After commenting about an unbelieving generation, Jesus cast out the demon. Later the disciples asked Him, "Why could we not cast it out?" (Mark 9:28). His response provides significant insight that we must not ignore if we desire to be effective in the spiritual war that rages in the unseen realm. Jesus said, "This kind cannot be driven out by anything but prayer" (Mark 9:20). Some manuscripts add "and fasting." In other words, the disciples lacked spiritual effectiveness because more prayer and fasting was needed.

Authority wasn't the problem. These guys belonged to Jesus, and they'd heard lots of powerful teaching and preaching. Even with that, they were spiritually ineffective in this particular battle.

What's the point? Peter, James, and John had witnessed the glory of the transfigured Christ. For a moment, they glimpsed the supernatural power and magnificence of the Lord. Then they came down from the mountaintop only to immediately witness an example of the spiritual warfare that constantly rages. They went from the glory of the Lord to the gory brokenness of the world. They learned that prayer is the way to witness the glory of God in the here and now.

They were called back to ministry and were taught a powerful lesson about ministry success. Does prayer matter in the spiritual battle? Does prayer matter for your family?

Does prayer matter for your church? Emphatically, Jesus said yes!

Prayer and fasting are essential to spiritual effectiveness. Is it possible that a lack of prayer and fasting in your life is leaving you spiritually ineffective and defeated by the enemy?

Questions for Reflection

1. What do you think of this father's statement: "I believe; help my unbelief"?

2. In Ephesians 6, the apostle Paul warns believers about spiritual warfare. What are we instructed there to do?

27

Miracle: Temple Tax in a Fish's Mouth

Read Matthew 17:24-27

A cartoon-like picture of a fish with a coin in its mouth can be found in classic children's Bible storybooks as an illustration of Matthew 17:24-27. While that simple picture is an accurate depiction of the miracle, it does not convey the deeper spiritual meaning of the surrounding story:

> When they came to Capernaum, the collectors of the two-drachma tax went up to Peter and said, "Does your teacher not pay the tax?" He said, "Yes." And when he came into the house, Jesus spoke to him first, saying, "What do you think, Simon? From whom do kings of the earth take toll or tax? From their sons or from others?" And when he said, "From others," Jesus said to him, "Then the sons are free. However, not to give offense to them, go to the sea and cast a hook and take the first fish that comes up, and when you open its mouth you will find a shekel. Take that and give it to them for me and for yourself." (Matthew 17:24-27)

When asked if Jesus paid the temple tax, Peter said yes. The following conversation with Jesus makes one wonder if Peter might have been making an assumption. Regardless, when Peter entered the house, Jesus was clearly aware of the conversation that had transpired on the outside.

The answer to Jesus's question was that kings don't tax their children. The implication is that Jesus, being the Son of God, was free from the temple tax. A deeper implication is that those who've placed faith in Jesus are also sons and daughters of God, and as such, are also free from the temple tax.

The temple tax was first established by God, as we read in Exodus 30:11-16. The temple tax requirement was a part of Old Testament law. Over time, this tax gradually increased to two drachma for every Jewish man.

So as not to offend those collecting the tax, Jesus instructed Peter to go fishing and to use a hook and line rather than a net. Jesus told Peter to look in the mouth of the first fish he caught and find a coin in its mouth. The coin would be enough to pay the tax for both Peter and Jesus.

A coin in the mouth of a fish seems a strange way to meet a need. While Jesus's instructions might sound absurd, Peter had previously been an up-close and personal witness to another miracle involving a catch of many more fish (Luke 5:1-11). I find it reassuring to see how Jesus used Peter's vocation as the vehicle for a step of faith. He instructed Peter to do what Peter knew how to do. The result was supernatural blessing.

Jesus not only knew the need without being told, He provided the exact amount of the need at the precise time the need arose. Praise to Jehovah Jireh—the God who provides!

Questions for Reflection

1. Jesus didn't want to give offense concerning the temple tax, but He wasn't concerned about giving offense in regard to healing on the Sabbath. What's the difference? (The answer is found in what Jesus said to Peter.)

2. What lesson was Jesus providing Peter (and us) in the way He met the need for the tax?

2 8

Miracle: Jesus Heals a Crippled Woman

Read Luke 13:10-17

The woman arrived at the synagogue bent over and unable to stand straight. For eighteen years she had walked with her face toward the ground, unable to look up.

Her name isn't given, and nothing is said about her family or friends. No details are shared regarding how she made a living. We know nothing significant about this woman except that she was in the synagogue on the Sabbath. The ruler of the synagogue had no regard for her, and he was indignant about Jesus freeing the woman from her suffering, because He did this on the Sabbath. Would this synagogue ruler have responded differently if the woman had been someone of high social status?

Jesus exposed the ruler's hypocrisy when He pointed out how the priest would water his animals on the Sabbath but wouldn't show compassion for a "daughter of Abraham" whom Satan had bound for eighteen years (Luke 13:15-16). The priest valued boundaries and rules more than compassion. For him, the law trumped mercy. Sadly and unbelievably, some people, even today, show more compassion for animals than for other human beings.

Luke, a physician, tells us that the woman's painful disability was caused by a "disabling spirit" (Luke 13:11). Her illness stemmed from a spiritual attack. Can you imagine the constant pain from her bent spine, and the challenges she faced in even minor tasks?

Jesus looked at the woman, and the first words out of His mouth were these: "Woman, you are freed from your disability" (Luke 13:12). When Jesus touched the woman, she immediately straightened up and began glorifying God.

The woman in this story is a picture of people in spiritual bondage. Was she worthy of the compassion Jesus showed her? Did she deserve to be set free? Did she merit His supernatural touch and gracious mercy of Jesus?

Merit is not a prerequisite for compassion. This is great news! Grace is receiving from Jesus what cannot be earned. Grace is receiving goodness and compassion that aren't deserved. Grace is receiving compassion in spite of the boundaries others often put in place.

If this woman showed up at your church, would compassion trump your boundaries? Is Jesus welcome to show His grace to those in bondage?

Jesus shows us unfathomable grace:

For one will scarcely die for a righteous person—though perhaps for a good person one would dare even to die—but God shows his love for us in that while we were still sinners, Christ died for us. (Romans 5:7-8)

He offers grace we could never earn:

For by grace you have been saved through faith. And this is not your own doing; it is the gift of God, not a result of works, so that no one may boast. (Ephesians 2:8-9)

Questions for Reflection

1. What are some personal boundaries that might keep you from showing the compassionate love of Christ to others?

2. The woman apparently continued to attend worship even though she'd suffered for eighteen years. What does this say about her faithfulness to God?

3. The woman suffered from "a disabling spirit." She was bound by Satan. Was the ruler of the synagogue bound by Satan in any way?

29

Miracle: Jesus Heals a Man of Dropsy on the Sabbath

Read Luke 14:1-14

Jesus had constant conflict with the Pharisees over a variety of issues. He harshly condemned them because of their hypocrisy, greed, and wickedness (Matthew 23). In light of this ongoing enmity between them, why did they invite Him to dinner (Luke 11:37-52)—and why did He accept their invitation?

The circumstances of the dinner, which was held on the Sabbath, point to the Pharisees having an agenda beyond fellowship with Jesus. Obviously, their invitation wasn't extended out of goodwill. Not only does Luke tell us that the Pharisees were watching Jesus, but it seems they purposely placed a man in front of Jesus who suffered from abnormal swelling in his body (Luke 14:2).

As was usually the case, Jesus wasted little time getting straight to the point. He asked them, "Is it lawful to heal on the Sabbath or not?" (14:3). While they "remained silent,"

Jesus healed the man and sent him on his way (14:4). Notice that the Pharisees made no argument about whether the man was genuinely healed.

Jesus had done exactly what the Pharisees expected, and now the Pharisees had an opportunity to fulfill their agenda. Right? Wrong. Jesus turned the tables by asking the Pharisees, "Which of you, having a son or ox that has fallen into a well on the Sabbath, will not immediately pull him out?" (14:5) Luke tells us that the Pharisees "could not reply to these things" (14:6). Surely they would express joy at the man's healing! But no—they didn't say a word.

The Pharisees weren't the least bit concerned about the man with dropsy. He was simply an object or tool to be used for justifying their condemnation of Jesus. Jesus, on the other hand, showed compassion for the man. Not only that, Jesus also showed compassion for the Pharisees by warning them and providing them another opportunity to respond to His unfathomable grace.

Jesus was now in charge of the agenda. He used the theme of dinners and invitations to reveal what would happen to those who reject His invitation. After observing the guests selecting their places at the table, Jesus first addressed the importance of humility:

> When you are invited by someone to a wedding feast, do not sit down in a place of honor, lest someone more distinguished than you be invited by him, and he who invited you both will come and say to you, "Give your place to this person," and then you will begin with shame to take the lowest place. (14:8-9)

Jesus moved on from there to discuss charity, as He addressed the host who had invited Him:

> When you give a dinner or a banquet, do not invite your friends or your brothers or your relatives or rich neighbors, lest they also invite you in return and you be repaid. But when you give a feast, invite the poor, the crippled, the lame, the blind, and you will be blessed, because they cannot repay you. For you will be repaid at the resurrection of the just. (14:12-14)

Where do you sit when invited to dinner? Who do you invite when you host a dinner? The Pharisees invited Jesus to dinner in hopes of advancing their agenda of condemnation and self-righteousness. Jesus accepted the invitation for the purpose of displaying compassion and teaching about humility and charity. He accepted the invitation so that He might offer His enemies one more chance to turn to Him in faith.

Questions for Reflection

1. Why didn't the Pharisees reply to Jesus's question regarding healing on the Sabbath?

2. Jesus noticed how the dinner guests "chose the places of honor." What did Jesus say regarding people who exalt themselves? When will this happen?

3. Who should we invite to dinner?

3 0

Miracle: Jesus Cleanses Ten Lepers

Read Luke 17:11-19

Bluetooth technology allows electronic devices to communicate without cables. (Bluetooth technology, by the way, was named for a second-century king of Denmark, Harald Bluetooth, who united Scandinavia.) Mobile phones can be connected wirelessly to laptops, radios, and audio speakers. Bluetooth technology bridges gaps and unites equipment that a few years ago required expensive cables.

The next miracle of Jesus reveals the importance of bridging a gap. As Jesus traveled from Galilee to Jerusalem, He was met by ten lepers on the outskirts of a village. The lepers shouted from a distance: "Jesus, Master, have mercy on us" (Luke 17:12). In that day, anyone with an infectious skin disease was required to stay away from other people and to announce their presence whenever anyone without leprosy came near. Since the lepers couldn't come near to Jesus, they cried out from a distance. Keep in mind that throughout the Bible, leprosy is a metaphor for sin.

Luke doesn't say how these pitiful outcasts with open running sores and rotting flesh knew about Jesus, but they'd undoubtedly heard of His miracles. Picture the scene in your mind. Jesus stood with His disciples facing ten men with leprosy. Scripture doesn't reveal how far apart they stood, but since the lepers had to call out in a loud voice to be heard, it was likely a significant gap. What a scene! These hopeless and diseased people were calling out because they couldn't draw close to the One having power to cleanse and heal.

Another wide gap is present in this story. After the lepers begged Jesus for mercy, He instructed them, "Go and show yourselves to the priests" (17:14). The second gap is seen in the distance between how Jesus responded to the lepers' plea for mercy, and how the lepers in turn responded to His command. Jesus didn't say, "You are healed." He gave them instructions to proceed as if they already were healed.

These lepers must have been Jewish. All Jews knew that outcast people who believed their skin disease to be in remission were required to present themselves to the priests. The lepers had to deduce that this command from Jesus meant healing. Jesus bridged a gap by sending His cleansing and life-giving healing to the lepers, yet they had to take the step of obedience, which they did: "And as they went, they were cleansed" (17:14). By the way, the size of the gap didn't matter. No matter how wide the gap, Jesus can cover the distance.

Can you imagine the expressions of happiness as these guys realized their leprosy was gone? Surely they were jumping, laughing, and shouting for joy! Perhaps they were moved to tears as they thought about being reunited with spouses, children, and friends. In those moments, maybe all they could think about was getting back to their former lives. At least, that's what nine of the lepers seemed to be thinking.

But one healed leper had other thoughts. He was moved to express his gratitude, now that Jesus had bridged the gap: "Then one of them, when he saw that he was healed, turned back, praising God with a loud voice; and he fell on his face at Jesus's feet, giving him thanks. Now he was a Samaritan" (Luke 17:15-16). One leper fell at the feet of Jesus in gratefulness. The others lepers were caught up in getting back to life.

I want to relate to the leper who turned back rather than the ones who didn't stop to express gratitude. Unfortunately, at times I find I'm more like the nine. We should be grateful that the Master had made His forgiveness and cleansing available through His shed blood at Calvary. Before we draw near to Him, we must recognize that like the ten lepers, we have a disease only Jesus can cleanse. We must cry out for mercy. When we do, Jesus bridges the gap.

Questions for Reflection

1. What point was Jesus making when He asked, "Was no one found to return and give praise to God except this foreigner?"

2. What is the significance of this statement: "As they went they were cleansed"?

3 1

Miracle: Jesus Raises Lazarus from the Dead

Read John 11:1-45

I have a number of friends who watch the popular television show *The Walking Dead*. I tried an episode but just couldn't get into it. My friends say they watch for the drama. I find that funny, yet I can't point a judging finger because I also temporarily suspend rational thought and enjoy weird, bizarre, and totally unreal stories. I guess I'm not a deadhead; zombie stories aren't my thing. But there's a story I like that's found in Scripture about a guy who died, decayed, and then came back to life. The very first "walking dead" story is found in the Bible.

Before looking into this story, I'll say a word about decay. A decaying body demonstrates no possibility for resuscitation (except for zombies).

When Jesus received word that His friend Lazarus was ill, He waited two days before making His way to Bethany, the home of Lazarus and his sisters (John 11:6). During this delay, Lazarus died. By the time Jesus finally arrived on the scene, four days had passed. The fourth day was considered the time when a dead body was absolutely certain to have entered a state of decay or putrefaction.

Understandably, Mary and Martha, the sisters of Lazarus, were heartbroken and disappointed. Martha didn't mince words. Seeing Jesus, she said to Him, "Lord, if you had been here, my brother would not have died. But even now I know that whatever you ask from God, God will give you" (11:21-22). Martha seemed to express faith that Lazarus might still live, yet when Jesus told her that Lazarus would rise again, Martha answered, "I know that he will rise again in the resurrection on the last day" (11:24). Her sister Mary also believed that if Jesus had arrived earlier, Lazarus wouldn't have died.

Although Jesus had raised others from the dead, no one believed that Jesus could raise a man to life who had been dead four days. Martha and Mary were disillusioned, torn, and confused.

Notice the compassion of Jesus. Twice in the story we're told how Jesus was deeply moved. At one point, He wept (11:35). He did this even knowing that He was about to raise Lazarus from the dead.

When Jesus arrived at the tomb, He commanded that the stone covering the tomb's entrance be removed (11:39). Martha, mindful of reality, responded, "Lord, by this time there will be an odor, for he has been dead four days" (11:39). Martha was saying, "Jesus, not even You can fix this. The situation is hopeless."

But Jesus, in a loud voice, called for Lazarus to come out—and Lazarus emerged from the tomb in his grave clothes.

With this miracle, Jesus left no doubt that He has authority over death and life. We can trust His promises of a future resurrection and life eternal. We can also take comfort in knowing that Jesus has great compassion, and He can bring goodness into our lives. Problems that seem impossible are not impossible for Jesus.

Questions for Reflection

1. Why did Jesus weep?

2. What might people have said if Jesus had raised Lazarus before the fourth day?

3. In His prayer, Jesus stated His reason for performing this miracle. What was it?

32

Miracle: Jesus Restores Sight to Bartimaeus

Read Matthew 20:29-34; Mark 10:46-52; Luke 18:35-43

Blind Bartimaeus sat by a dusty road begging from those who passed by. Every day he depended on the generosity and compassion of others for his survival. He sat in an area near the old city of Jericho where hundreds of years before, Joshua and the Israelites experienced a monumental miracle. Joshua 6 tells the story of Israel's conquest of Jericho. In faith and obedience, the Israelites marched around the walls of Jericho as they'd been instructed by Yahweh. When the Israelites finished with shouts and the sound of trumpets, the walls around the city collapsed. The Israelites enjoyed their first victory in the land of promise.

Unfortunately, the earthly land of promise would never become a place of peace and rest because of the spiritual blindness of the Israelites.

As Jesus neared the end of His earthly ministry, He was walking in the footsteps of Joshua. Passing through Jericho, Jesus was on the threshold of achieving a victory that would open the way to the ultimate place of promise. Through His death and resurrection, Jesus was about to open the way for all who believe.

Jesus, the prophesied Son of David, was being followed by a crowd of people. Bartimaeus heard the noise of the crowd and wanted to know what was going on. When he was told that Jesus of Nazareth was passing by, Bartimaeus began to shout: "Jesus, Son of David, have mercy on me!" (Luke 18:38). This scene was symbolic of Jesus bypassing those who are blind to their true need. The only one to cry out for mercy was the one who recognized his blindness.

Even when rebuked by the crowd, Bartimaeus cried out "all the more" (18:39). He had a fervent faith that wouldn't give in to loud voices of opposition. Unfortunately, many believers today acquiesce to the crowd and shy away from living boldly for Christ.

This physically blind beggar used a Messianic title to call out to Jesus. Bartimaeus let everyone know he believed Jesus was the Messiah who could grant mercy. In the midst of a people who ultimately rejected Jesus as God's Son, there sat a blind man who had to beg to survive. Unlike those who possessed physical sight, this man possessed spiritual sight, which allowed him to see that Jesus has both the power to heal and the compassion to grant mercy.

The plea of Bartimaeus got the attention of Jesus, who asked Bartimaeus, "What do you want me to do for you?" (Luke 18:41) Bartimaeus asked for his sight to be restored, and Jesus granted his request. Jesus said to Bartimaeus (so that everyone could hear), "Your faith has made you well" (Luke 18:42).

Before I came to know Christ, I was much like Bartimaeus. I was a blind beggar. Fortunately, many years ago, Jesus approached me in the form of a pastor who shared the gospel. I accepted Christ, and He met my greatest need. He forgave me of my sin and granted me eternal life.

Maybe Christ is passing near you as you read about His signs and wonders. Have you asked Jesus to heal you of spiritual blindness?

Questions for Reflection

1. How did Bartimaeus respond to having his sight restored?

2. How might possessions, relationships, or situations prevent people from seeing their need to turn to Christ?

33

Miracle: Jesus Withers the Fig Tree

Read Matthew 21:18-22; Mark 11:12-14; Mark 11:20-25

The cursing of a fig tree is one of the most unusual miracles of Jesus. The event occurred on Monday morning of the week leading up to His crucifixion. As Jesus and His disciples made their way from Bethany to Jerusalem, Jesus saw a fig tree with leaves. He inspected the tree for fruit, and when He found none, He spoke to the tree: "May no one ever eat fruit from you again" (Mark 11:14).

The following day, when Jesus and the disciples passed by the tree again, Peter remarked, "Rabbi, look! The fig tree that you cursed has withered" (11:21).

Many theologians point to the symbolism of Jesus coming to the end of His earthly ministry, inspecting Israel, and finding no fruit. This conclusion is supported by Old Testament passages where the fig tree is a metaphor for Israel (Jeremiah 8:13; Hosea 9:10; Joel 1:17). Some scholars also suggest that the tree in this miracle is symbolic of people who appear to be fruitful—like the religious rulers—but who are lacking in any real fruit.

In addition to these symbolic messages, we have the response of Jesus to the disciples, who were surprised by the tree's condition. They asked Jesus, "How did the fig tree wither at once?" (Matthew 21:20). Jesus answered,

> Have faith in God. Truly, I say to you, whoever says to this mountain, "Be taken up and thrown into the sea," and does not doubt in his heart, but believes that what he says will come to pass, it will be done for him. Therefore I tell you, whatever you ask in prayer, believe that you have received it, and it will be yours. And whenever you stand praying, forgive, if you have anything against anyone, so that your Father also who is in heaven may forgive you your trespasses. (Mark 11:22-25)

While the disciples were staring at the fig tree that withered because of its lack of fruitfulness, Jesus drew their attention to faith and prayer. Faith and prayer are essential to living a life of fruitfulness for God.

Jesus addressed the importance of faith by using the metaphor of moving a mountain. Even what seems impossible is possible with faith.

Fruitfulness in prayer is dependent on believing and a willingness to forgive others.

I can't stress enough the importance of interpreting Scripture with Scripture. These verses on prayer and faith must be considered in light of many other Bible passages.

For example, included in the model prayer that Jesus taught His disciples are these words: "Your kingdom come. Your will be done, on earth as it is in heaven" (Matthew 6:10).

We must also consider this instruction from the apostle John:

> And this is the confidence that we have toward him, that if we ask anything according to his will he hears us. And if we know that he hears us in whatever we ask, we know that we have the requests that we have asked of him. (1 John 5:14-15)

When we ask that God's will be done, we're implicitly asking that our wills be set aside for His will. What God desires to accomplish is much better than anything we desire or can envision.

Questions for Reflection

1. When Jesus inspects your fruitfulness—what does He find?

2. Are your prayers characterized by faith and a desire to see God's will accomplished?

34

Miracle: Jesus Heals a Servant's Severed Ear

Read Luke 22:47-53

With this miracle we've arrived at the darkest time of Jesus's earthly life, and events are moving rapidly. The agonizing prayers of Jesus in the garden of Gethsemane, His betrayal by Judas, and His arrest tend to overshadow the healing of a servant. Peter's attack on the High Priest's servant—and that servant's subsequent healing—happened quickly. Neither Luke nor John dwell upon the healing in their narratives.

Jesus had finished praying in Gethsemane only to find His disciples sleeping (Luke 22:45). Moments later, a crowd arrived to apprehend Jesus. Judas, who was leading them, approached Jesus to kiss Him. Jesus said to him, "Judas, would you betray the Son of Man with a kiss?" (23:48). One disciple was betraying Jesus while the others were sleeping during His moment of need. And in these moments, Jesus of course was fully aware that in the coming hours He would suffer indescribable pain from beatings, scourging, being nailed to a cross, and having the sin of the entire world pressed upon Him.

Seeing Jesus being betrayed and arrested, Peter turned to the sword and cut off the ear of the High Priest's servant, whose name was Malchus (John 18:10). But Jesus demonstrated loving restraint. Matthew tells us than in these moments, Jesus asked His disciples, "Do you think that I cannot appeal to my Father, and he will at once send me more than twelve legions of angels?" (Matthew 26:53). I'm glad He didn't call upon His angels in that moment, because if He had, we would have lost our only way to God.

In the moments before the crowd had arrived, Jesus had prayed for the removal of the cup He was about to drink, yet He chose to continue on the path toward Calvary (Luke 22:42). Jesus told Peter to put away the sword, and He said, "Shall I not drink the cup that the Father has given me?" His desire was to do the will of the Father, and His love was for lost sinners.

In spite of His intense disappointment and grief, Jesus stopped to heal the servant's ear that Peter had cut off. Nothing indicated that this servant was a follower of Jesus or had in any way expressed faith in Jesus. In fact, he was accompanying those who opposed Jesus. The last miracle of Jesus, before He went to the cross to die for the sins of others, was to lovingly heal a person who was His enemy.

The healing of Malchus demonstrates Christ's love for all people. We see in this miracle a beautiful picture of unfathomable love and amazing grace.

Questions for Reflection

1. What was wrong with how Peter attempted to defend Jesus? What do we learn from the way Jesus responded to this?

2. According to 1 Peter 2:18-25, what did Peter eventually learn?

3. Why do followers of Christ struggle with the way of suffering?

35

Miracle: Another Miraculous Catch of Fish

Read John 21:4-11

John 21 is a favorite chapter in the Bible for many people. Since the events recorded there occur after Christ's resurrection, some people might argue that the most important aspect of this chapter is the appearance of Jesus on the shore; this was His third appearance to the disciples after He arose. Other people might be drawn in this chapter to the loving restoration of Peter by the Lord. While both of these are highly significant and moving, it's the miraculous catch of fish that's considered the true miracle in this chapter, and the last one performed by Christ before He ascended to the Father.

If this miracle seems familiar to you, it's because this was the second time the disciples—with guidance from Jesus—hauled in a huge catch of fish. The first occurrence is recorded in Luke 5:1-11. After that first miraculous catch, Jesus had said to Peter, "Do not be afraid; from now on you will be catching men" (Luke 5:10).

Jesus then spent three years preparing these men for what was to come once He returned to the Father. Later, after the disciples were empowered by the Holy Spirit on the day of Pentecost, they would become powerful witnesses and founders of the church. On this particular day, however, the disciples had gone back to their old occupation—not fishing for men, but fishing for fish. Even though they'd seen the resurrected Jesus, they displayed no sense of mission or vision for the future. They seemed to have forgotten Jesus's words to Peter: "And I tell you, you are Peter, and on this rock I will build my church, and the gates of hell shall not prevail against it" (Matthew 16:18).

In fact, I find it surprising they didn't recognize Jesus as soon as He told them to cast their net on the right side of the boat. Talk about déjà vu! Once the net began to fill, John recognized Jesus, and told Peter, "It is the Lord!" (John 21:7). Peter didn't wait for the boat to get to shore; he dived immediately into the water so He could quickly get to Jesus.

Once their breakfast on the shore with Jesus was over, Jesus had an emotional conversation with Peter, instructing him to "feed my sheep" and to "follow me" (John 21:17,19).

This miracle serves as a powerful reminder of the future work Christ had for these men and all future disciples to accomplish. The work can be accomplished only under the direction and empowerment of Jesus. He would soon give

His followers a command that has come to be known as the Great Commission:

> All authority in heaven and on earth has been given to me. Go therefore and make disciples of all nations, baptizing them in the name of the Father and of the Son and of the Holy Spirit, teaching them to observe all that I have commanded you. And behold, I am with you always, to the end of the age. (Matthew 28:18-20)

> You will receive power when the Holy Spirit has come upon you, and you will be my witnesses in Jerusalem and in all Judea and Samaria, and to the end of the earth. (Acts 1:8)

We've been called to be witnesses and disciple-makers. We don't go in our own strength but in the power of the Holy Spirit. The final miracle of Jesus prior to returning to the right hand of the Father was to remind us of His power and love. He goes with us and before us!

Glory to God. He is unfathomable!

Questions for Reflection

1. Are you actively working to accomplish the Great Commission?

2. Are you seeking to follow Christ and feed His sheep?

3. In what ways will you become active as a disciple-maker?

Made in the USA
Columbia, SC
25 February 2020